ES
PSYCHOLOGY
General Editor
Peter Herriot

=A5=

INFORMATION AND SKILL

ESSENTIAL

PSYCHOLOGY

INFORMATION AND SKILL

**David Legge and
Paul J. Barber**

Methuen

First published in 1976 by Methuen & Co Ltd
11 New Fetter Lane, London EC4P 4EE
© 1976 David Legge and Paul J. Barber
Printed in Great Britain by
Richard Clay (The Chaucer Press), Ltd
Bungay, Suffolk

ISBN (hardback) 0 416 84060 4
ISBN (paperback) 0 416 84070 1

We are grateful to Grant McIntyre of
Open Books Publishing Ltd
for assistance in the preparation of this series.

Contents

Preface

Behaviour is composed of sequences of movements. Some of them are habitual, serving no obvious purpose. Most, however, are tailored to circumstance, executed for an explicit purpose, to achieve an evident goal. The study of these 'voluntary' movements and acts is the study of perceptual-motor skills. The importance of skill is fundamental. Without it one could not move, manipulate or speak. It is the critical link between man and his environment since it is through the exercise of skill that he meets his needs.

The importance of understanding skill is not only because without it we are in danger of providing elegant accounts of decision-making, problem-solving and language while making no provision for how we manage to move at all. It is also plausible to propose that these more complex mental activities have evolved from those which subserve bodily skills (Bartlett, 1958). If this view is valid, an understanding of the processes underlying perceptual-motor skill may provide a basis for understanding such complex and puzzling mental phenomena.

In this book we have tried to bring together ideas about the nature of the processes underlying skill. Sometimes this has involved reinterpretation of 'classic' findings and in the final chapter some speculations about a model for skill are presented. A definitive statement is impossible at this time but we hope this volume will lay a foundation for building an understanding of this aspect of behaviour.

We doubt that any of you will become better cricketers,

knitters or typists as a result of reading this book, but we shall have succeeded in no small measure if you find more interest than before in the behaviour around you (including your own). Familiarity, they say, breeds contempt; skill, the faithful servant, goes on providing a near faultless, inconspicuous service year after year. We here attempt to accord it some overdue recognition.

Later we shall show how important feedback systems are for stabilizing performance. Our feedback system was Hilary Klee, without whose continued encouragement and inspiration this book might never have seen the light of day.

Our words were deciphered by those virtuosi of transcription skill, Patricia Caple and Valerie Elliott.

Editor's Introduction

Perceptual-motor skills are important for at least two reasons. First, they are a necessary condition for the execution of almost every sort of plan. As David Legge and Paul Barber point out, the brilliance of a chess move can only be actualized if the piece is moved from one position to another on the board. Second, perceptual-motor skills are a prime example of the person acting upon his environment and modifying his subsequent actions as a result of the effects of his previous ones. Legge and Barber take us through such theoretical problems as whether we can use more than one channel for processing information at any one point in time, with the help of such diverse characters as cricketers, an amicable drunk, and Tom and Jerry.

This book belongs to Unit A of *Essential Psychology*. What unifies the titles in this unit is the notion of the human being as a processor of information. Like a computer we can register information, code it, perform operations on the coded version, store the result, and subsequently retrieve it. Moreover, like a computer, we can use our output, or behaviour, as feedback or evidence by which to monitor our subsequent performance. The authors in Unit A are more concerned with making generalizations about people than with exploring their individual differences. Further, they deal with personal mental processes rather than with interpersonal social processes. They also probably place more stress on the traditional scientific experiment as a source of evidence than do most of the authors of the other units. However, the computer analogy may not be suitable for handling other situations, where there is no immediate sensory experience or no easily identifiable consequent behaviour. And some psychologists also feel that it detracts from the concept of the individual as a person who can consciously act upon and control his environment. The reader will find other general conceptual frameworks in other units. Psychology is struggling to do justice to the complexities of its subject matter; it is hardly likely to find any single analogy to encompass the richness of human behaviour and experience. Coming to terms with a variety of explanatory frameworks may decrease our confidence in psychology as a mature science; but perhaps it is best that we should be honest about what we don't know.

Essential Psychology as a whole is designed to reflect the changing structure and function of psychology. The authors are both academics and professionals, and their aim has been to introduce the most important concepts in their areas to beginning students. They have tried to do so clearly, but have not attempted to conceal the fact that concepts that now appear central to their work may soon be peripheral. In other words, they have presented psychology as a developing set of views of man, not as a body of received truth. Readers are not intended to study the whole series in order to 'master the basics'. Rather, since different people may wish to use different theoretical frameworks for their own purposes, the series has been designed so that each title stands on its own. But it is possible that if the reader has read no psychology before, he will enjoy individual books more if he has read the introductions (A1, B1, etc.) to the units to which they belong. Readers of the units concerned with applications of psychology (E and F) may benefit from reading all the introductions.

A word about references in the text to the work of other writers – e.g. 'Smith, 1974'. These occur where the author feels he must acknowledge (by name) an important concept or some crucial evidence. The book or article referred to will be listed in the references (which double as name index) at the back of the book. The reader is invited to consult these sources if he wishes to explore topics further. A list of general further reading is also to be found at the back of this book.

We hope you enjoy psychology.

Peter Herriot

I
Introducing perceptual-motor skills

This book is about the most fundamental of all aspects of behaviour, perceptual-motor skill. It allows us to interact with the world, to manipulate it and to move about in it. It is the ability to coordinate muscular contractions in tune with the prevailing situation such that some deliberate change is brought about. All behaviour incorporates some element of perceptual-motor skill even when other more dramatic components are demonstrably more important. A chess master may make a brilliant move, for example. The brilliance of the move will be judged by the wisdom of making that move rather than any other. But, less obviously, in addition to the skill involved in selecting that particular move, the master has also exercised the perceptual-motor skill needed to move the chess piece at all. Without perceptual-motor skill the game cannot take place and the brilliant 'move' must remain imprisoned in the brain of the inventor. In short, without perceptual-motor skill our intentions can never become actions.

Perhaps it would be of little consequence if one could not play chess. However, the same essential skill is necessary in order to stay alive. It subserves eating and drinking, and the human race could hardly reproduce itself without it.

No account of any kind of behaviour can be adequate without including a perceptual-motor skills component. However, skills usually offer a quiet, efficient service which leaves them out of the limelight. They play their part so unobtrusively that often they are hardly noticed at all. That is, until something goes wrong and somehow what was intended doesn't happen after all. One wonders at, and is frustrated by, the lack of function instead of wondering at the marvels of voluntary movement.

We intend, in this book, to explore some of the problems and issues that arise in attempting to understand the processes which underlie perceptual-motor skill.

Characteristics of skill

It is necessary to distinguish what psychologists mean by skill since the word's typical use differs somewhat. The dictionary includes as a definition of skill the concept of 'practised' ability. It is generally considered that skill, unlike talent, is a consequence of training and practice. So a skilled worker is one who has been trained, perhaps over a prolonged period. There is the corollary that without such training performance of a skill is impossible.

The psychological concept of skill includes the notion of practised ability but is broader since it also includes untrained (though not necessarily unpractised) skills. The manipulatory skill of reaching for a glass of beer and draining it without spilling a drop is considered as much a skill as potting a black on the snooker table, knitting, and making bread. It is conceivable that even relatively complex behaviour patterns are genuinely unlearned, being completely determined by a 'wired-in' neural structure (walking is something like this), but it is safer to assume that there is a learned component even if it is not obvious.

It has been a feature of discussions about the nature of skill to distinguish skilled performance from the mere exercise of a habit. The critical feature that is usually stressed is that skills are adaptable and flexible while habits are executed blindly without reference to their consequences or appropriateness to particular circumstances. In other words, a skilled act is typified by achieving (or at least seeking to achieve) a particular end result, while a habit is simply a response without an end to justify or guide it.

The distinction may be highlighted in the behaviour of many sportsmen. It is very common for them to indulge in habitual responses which serve no discoverable purpose. For example, many bowlers and wicketkeepers can be recognized by the shuffles and chassés they produce before delivery or receiving

12

the ball. Similar redundant habits are observed among tennis players before serving. Some of these habitual rituals may serve the purpose of establishing a predictable behavioural baseline before launching the responses that actually matter, but there is a clear difference between habits of this kind and the skilled responses that the same sportsman makes in handling the ball, be it tennis or cricket. The main feature of this difference is that the skilled response is adjusted minutely to fit particular circumstances and to bring about a defined end result.

A vivid example of the flexible and adaptive nature of skilled behaviour is provided by Johnson (1961). He relates the story of 'The Woodchopper's Ball', a contest between two woodmen, both highly skilled axemen. All sorts of tests were devised to assess their speed, accuracy and even style. They were judged equal on all counts until the chief examiner decreed that in the final task each should chop with the other man's axe. The champion proved able to chop better with his opponent's axe than could the runner-up. The tie was broken by the emphasis upon adaptability that this final task imposed.

Laboratory tasks for studying skill

Laboratory tasks have been devised for the study of this kind of behaviour. These are tasks which permit the experimenter to pose a controlled problem to the subject and also permit the subject's performance to be carefully measured. Some of these tasks bear an obvious relation to the real life situation from which they were derived but most are deliberately artificial. Their purpose is to permit the study of the essence of real life skills. To achieve this end it is often necessary to define a task which stresses only some of the underlying mechanisms that are normally mobilized in skilled performance.

These tasks divide into two main groups, those which require relatively imprecise ungraded responses and those which demand precise graded responses. The former are particularly convenient when the research is aimed at discovering how fast the subject can choose to make a response, while the latter have to be used when one is concerned with how subjects control their responses accurately.

Although many real life situations such as steering a car or playing darts demand very accurate response control, there are a number which can be performed successfully even though the spatial accuracy of responses is not great. For example, typewriting demands only that the correct key is struck. On a standard typewriter a spatial error of as much as 1 cm will still permit 'error-free' behaviour in terms of what is typed on the page. As we shall see later, there is a trading relationship between speed and accuracy so that if a response has to be made very quickly the task should be so designed that small errors in accuracy are tolerated. An illustration of this principle is tennis or squash. The racquet head has an area several times larger than the ball. This permits a satisfactory 'hit' even though the ball does not strike the centre of the racquet. In this type of game the speed of the oncoming missile is such that continuous play would be impossible if the racquet head were reduced to, say, one-tenth of its area.

Ungraded response tasks – reaction times

Ungraded response tasks are also called reaction time tasks since what is measured is the time elapsing between the task being presented to the subject and the subject initiating his chosen response. This time is called the *latency* of the response. It is thought that most of this time is taken up with preparation of the response about to be made. When this is the only thing to be measured (except to note whether the subject chooses the correct response or not) then it is obviously convenient to design a task which will expose this 'response preparation' latency most clearly. For this reason many experimenters prefer to conduct experiments in which the latency of each discrete (distinct) response is separately measured. This has the advantage of ensuring that the stimulus conditions associated with a particular latency are unequivocal.

Graded response tasks – aiming and tracking

Tasks devised to study graded responses may be divided into two forms. They are target aiming tasks and target acquisition tasks. In these tasks the essential criterion of success is the spatial accuracy achieved. They are usually devised so that only very small errors are tolerated. A great many everyday situations provide examples of such emphasis upon accuracy. Some of them also stress timing either in terms of minimum latency or, more often, in terms of optimum latency. Steering a car offers an excellent example of the latter. The angle through

14

which the steering wheel is turned is critical, but it also matters *when* the wheel is turned. The correct angle of turn a second or two too early or too late could be as catastrophic as the wrong deflection executed at the right time.

Aiming tasks are perhaps the simplest of the graded responses. By definition, there is a discrete target at which the subject aims. Some games are based upon aiming tasks. Two that are traditionally played in English pubs are darts and shove-ha'penny. (The association of aiming tasks with alcohol might be a topic for some psycho-sociological research!) Other non-sporting examples are hammering a nail, swatting a fly and cracking a boiled egg with a spoon.

There is psychological interest in aiming tasks because these tasks make observable the accuracy of the initial response undistorted by the addition of corrections made during the movement. We shall see later that there is good reason to conceive of all discrete responses as being essentially of this kind. It is often necessary, however, to devise special tasks in order to look at the mechanisms involved.

Target acquisition tasks while essentially similar to aiming tasks differ from them in one important respect. The subject is permitted to correct his initial response, usually without limit. They may be conceived of as comprising a series of aiming responses which terminates when the required accuracy is achieved. Everyday life is the best source of examples of target acquisition problems. It is only in the artificial context of contests that corrections are prohibited by anything except time. In driving a car, provided one chooses to go slowly enough, it is possible to correct an inappropriate steering wheel movement.

Tracking is a target acquisition task in which the target is continuously changing. In this way a continuously changing problem may be presented to the subject and, therefore, he is enjoined to respond continuously. We shall argue that, in fact, control is intermittent, and that it is not inappropriate to conceive of the tracking task as a series of aiming movements at a moving target. It would, however, be a gross over-simplification to assert that tracking was no more than that.

Compensatory and pursuit tracking. There are two kinds of tracking: compensatory and pursuit. Pursuit tracking is almost self-descriptive. Two indices or pointers are displayed to the subject; one is the target, say a continuously moving dot on a screen, and is controlled by the experimenter. The other index represents the subject's performance and alters only as a function of his control responses. This could be another dot on the screen directly controlled by the subject. In general his task is to keep the two indices superimposed. In a less technologically sophisticated era a pursuit tracking apparatus frequently incorporated a long strip of paper on which was drawn an irregular line. This strip passed behind a slot in a screen and so was visible to the subject who held a pencil and tried to keep its point on the moving wiggly line. In this simplest form the subject responds directly, but other equipment can be interposed between the subject and the object he manipulates so that his response may actually involve a variety of actions such as turning a wheel, pushing or pulling a lever or even moving a 'rudder-bar' with his feet. This kind of apparatus can be altered very simply to give the subject advance information about the course he has to track. The amount of advance information, or preview, can be varied by altering the width of the slot and the course speed. This apparatus represents a one-dimensional tracking task. It is difficult to extend this task to two dimensions without making use of an electronic display such as a cathode ray tube like that used in a television set. The electronic version permits two-dimensional tracking using a joy-stick or joy-ball (rolling ball) or even two independent control knobs or levers.

Pursuit tracking is a laboratory analogue of a large number of everyday situations. Once again steering a vehicle provides an obvious example but controlling machine tools and ironing a shirt are other examples.

Compensatory tracking differs from pursuit tracking in that there is only one changing index or moving pointer. This is influenced by both the perturbations imposed by the experimenter and the control responses made by the subject. The subject's job is to keep this index at a particular value. In visual compensatory tracking the moving index, for example an oscillating pointer on a dial, has to be held on a predetermined point.

In general, compensatory tracking is more difficult than pursuit tracking. The extra difficulty probably stems from the fact that the subject receives no direct indication of the effect of his responses on the display. It therefore takes him far longer to

16

learn the relations between his responses and changes in the display. Similarly, unless he stops responding altogether, he receives no uncontaminated, clear view of the movement of the target which he is trying to match and thus nullify. In consequence the subject's performance on compensatory tracking tends to lag behind the 'course' to a more marked extent than on a pursuit task.

Examples of compensatory tracking in everyday life are rarer than examples of pursuit tracking. Since it is essentially less efficient, that is not too surprising. However, some do exist. Steering a ship on a compass bearing is one such. The coxswain has to compensate for variations in wind and sea to maintain his course. Standing on one leg in a high wind is another example.

An outline model of the underlying processes

Welford (1958) suggested that the processes underlying behaviour of this kind could be divided into three major groups, acting sequentially. These were: input processes concerned with the interpretation of information, translation processes that essentially determine what needs to be done and output processes which implement behaviour patterns appropriate to those needs. It is evident that the central translation processes not only play a key role but also need to have access to two critical kinds of information. They need to 'know' what the overall and local goals are, and they need to have access to a store of information which allows them to select appropriate rather than inappropriate responses in order to achieve those goals.

In Figure 1.1 is depicted an attempt to specify the main stages in information processing which are necessary to permit skilled behaviour. This model is an elaboration of Welford's three-stage model.

The train of events that is envisaged runs as follows. For series of responses in which corrections can be made it is necessary to consider that the sequence operates repeatedly.

The most important overall function of the input mechanisms which inform the system about the state of the world and its relation to it, is to determine that the required state already exists or, if not, what changes are required to bring it about. Such a change is labelled a *required object modulation* (ROM).

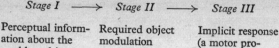

	Stage I $\longrightarrow$	Stage II $\longrightarrow$	Stage III
Input	Perceptual information about the world, and in particular about the spatial location of target and object	Required object modulation Proprioceptive information about the muscles and joints is also required	Implicit response (a motor programme)
	$\downarrow$	$\downarrow$	$\downarrow$
Output	The required object modulation, calculated to bring the object into correspondence with the target	The implicit response, a compact unit specifying in coded form the sequence of muscular changes calculated to be needed to bring about the required object modulation	An orderly series of signals distributed to the relevant muscles and patterned in time

Fig. 1.1 *A three-stage model of the principal processes underlying the performance of skill. The main inputs and outputs to each stage are summarized.*

The 'object' may be some particular feature of the immediate environment (including parts of the body) directly or indirectly controlled by the individual. The problem faced by the individual determines or defines what is the object in any particular situation. The task requires that this should be matched with a given target.

Let us take as an example the problem of drinking a pint of beer. An initial survey may establish that the said pint is located on a bar-top some several centimetres away and that one is standing in front of the bar with hands in pockets. The overall instruction, the goal, is to quaff the beer, but this goal requires the elaboration of an ordered set of sub-goals. The first of these is to grip the pint appropriately, preparatory to lifting it without spilling, raising it to the lips and then with co-ordinated action of lips, throat, arm and breathing, drink it. The initial acquisition of the pint on the bar will be a sufficient problem to show the mode of operation of the model.

In this example the target is the handle of the beer mug, and the object which has to be brought into conjunction with it is the hand. The initial survey establishes that target and object are not yet in correct relation to one another and, furthermore, since both are stationary, some modulation of or change in the object will be required to achieve this. It will not be sufficient to wait. There could be other circumstances, for example, where the hand is already in motion, and it could be predicted that providing the existing response patterns are allowed to proceed, the required state of affairs will eventually occur.

It is the primary function of the first stage of the model to define the required object modulation. This is done in the context of the information it receives about the relative spatial locations of target and object and the instructions it receives about the goal to be achieved.

The next problem is to determine a response or sequence of responses which will bring about this required object modulation. The system could function entirely by trial and error, each trial being a random selection from all possible responses. Setting aside pathology, we believe that this does not happen except possibly in very young infants. Although responses may be imperfect they are seldom very wide of the mark. It is therefore necessary to specify some way in which the output from the second stage of the model can be reasonably close to what is required. Two processes come to mind. The first, and potentially faster in operation, would be to select one out of a store of established connections (or associations) between required object modulations and the responses which have, in the past, produced them. The alternative scheme would involve a prediction mechanism (which itself would need access to such a store of connections) to check in advance each response, selected more or less at random, to see if it *would* have the desired effect. This prediction system would enable the response to be chosen using vicarious trial and error, that is by making internal predictions about the consequences of different responses and choosing that response which is predicted to be accurate.

The exact posture and the location of the object with respect to the individual are critical in determining whether a particular response would be satisfactory. It follows that if the store of relations between response and effect were to be in the form of a list of specific associations, an inordinately large amount of storage space would be required and the great majority of new situations would have to be dealt with in some other way. For example, explicit trial and error would be necessary because the vicarious approach involves prediction of the relative accuracy of each potential response. A more efficient arrangement which would permit effective generalization from experience to new, non-identical but similar situations, would be to have a store, not of specific associations, but of *functional rules*. The difference proposed here is comparable with the contrast between an account of language in terms of syntactical rules (Chomsky, 1959) rather than the operation of simple associative stimulus-response bonds (Skinner, 1957) (see A7).

Defining an efficient response depends upon information about the effectors (the muscles and joints), and about the relation between the effectors and the object which is to be modulated. In our drinking example this relation is trivial because the object (i.e. the hand) *is* the effector. In many other situations however, including racquet and bat games, and most laboratory tasks, the two are separate and a complex relation may intervene between them. The most useful direct source of information about the state of the effectors is *proprioception*. This is the sense which tells us where our limbs are when we cannot see them. In fact, many situations virtually force reliance on this sense because vision is busy elsewhere. Imagine playing tennis if one had to look at one's hands and feet before each stroke! The relation between the effectors and the object they affect is called the *control system dynamics*. These have to be learned by experience and are essentially the rules described above. Perhaps the main variety of learning that is called 'getting the feel of it' is learning these rules.

The output from the second stage (see Fig. 1.1) is not a response in the manifest observable sense but instead it is an *implicit response* (IR). The implicit response is a plan or programme which, if implemented, will define a sequence of muscular changes. A further stage intervenes between the implicit response and the real world. The main reason for introducing yet another stage is to handle the problem of time, and the difference in the size of psychological and physiological units of response. The psychological units tend to be either 'acts' or 'movements', while the physiological unit is in terms of muscle contractions. A temporally organized set of muscle twitches is required even to produce a simple movement and the physiological specification of an act is obviously even more complex. The final message which ultimately causes the act to occur has

20

to be in the language or code of muscular contractions. Therefore, a system must intervene to translate the demands of the implicit response into the reality of an orderly sequence of muscular changes. This relation between the implicit response and the observed output or behavioural response is similar to that between a cassette recording and the symphony that emerges from the loudspeaker of an appropriate cassette-player. The cassette is a unit which contains information about a sequence of events. When 'played' it defines 'behaviour' over an extended period of time.

The purpose of outlining this model of the processes underlying the performance of skills is to provide a structure within which studies of skilled behaviour can be incorporated. Particular tasks make heavier demands on some stages of processing than others. In the chapters to come we shall consider aspects of skill which reveal the characteristics of the hypothetical stages outlined here.

2
Timing mental processes

The reaction time (RT) experiment has its origins in the work of the physiologist Helmholtz (1850). This particular paradigm was invented rather by accident during the course of a series of experiments aimed at establishing the speed of conduction of information by nerves (see A2). He was working in the context of a general belief (which he questioned) that thoughts, presumably meditated by nerves, travelled at the speed of light, if not faster. He had the temerity to seek to test this dogma experimentally.

His first experiment was performed on an excised nerve-muscle preparation from a frog. Electrical stimulation of the nerve caused the muscle to twitch. Helmholtz recorded the time interval between stimulating the nerve close to the muscle and the subsequent twitch of the muscle (that is, the response latency). He also recorded the latency of the muscle twitch following stimulation applied at a distance from the muscle. He found that in the latter condition the response was delayed. By subtracting the shorter time from the longer he calculated the extra time due to the greater distance along the nerve that the stimulation had travelled. By dividing this distance by the extra time he calculated the conduction velocity. An updated version of this experiment, using electronic recording equipment, still features in most undergraduate courses in physiology.

Although this experiment showed quite clearly that nerve conduction rates in the nerve-muscle preparation were far slower than the speed of light, the experiment could be criticized as misleading. After all, the frog was dead and the nerve in question was a motor nerve. It was conceivable that sensory nerves might have different properties. In seeking a paradigm for the study of sensory nerve conduction in live human subjects, Helmholtz invented the reaction time experiment.

The similarity with the frog experiment is immediately obvious. The human subject was stimulated with a weak electric current applied either to the elbow or to the wrist. He was instructed to press a key with his other hand as soon as he felt the shock. As before, Helmholtz planned to find the difference in the response latency associated with different sites of stimulation and, knowing the distance between the sites, calculate the conduction velocity of sensory nerves. In some experiments Helmholtz obtained figures which implied velocities of the order of 100 metres per second, a figure which is comparable with calculations based on more exact modern experiments. However, Helmholtz never felt satisfied with these data because on some occasions he recorded faster responses to the more distant stimulus.

This paradigm of Helmholtz was essentially a simple reaction time experiment. The stimulus was predictable in quality though not in time of arrival and there was no ambiguity about the response that had to be made to it. The first thing that strikes one about this experiment is that whereas simple reaction times may be of the order of 200 milliseconds in duration (one-fifth of a second), less than 10 per cent of that time can be accounted for in terms of conduction along peripheral nerves. The great bulk of time is spent inside the brain, presumably on the problem of deciding whether or not to respond.

Decomposing decision times

Shortly after Helmholtz' invention of the simple reaction time experiment Donders (1868) elaborated the paradigm and described three different sorts of reaction time experiments. He called them the 'a', 'b' and 'c' reactions, and set out to show how by using them it would be possible to calculate the time taken up by particular mental processes – a truly ambitious aim when the processes themselves were only the products of plausible inference.

Donders' 'a' reaction was a *simple reaction time* task similar to that developed by Helmholtz. Donders used a slightly different version in which subjects responded vocally to a stimulus which they heard. The 'b' reaction was a *choice reaction time* task in which the stimulus was one of five possible sounds, and the subject was instructed to mimic that sound in his response. The 'c' reaction was rather like a compromise between these two. The stimulus could be any one of five possible sounds but the subject was instructed to respond to only one of them. This reaction is also called a 'go–no go' reaction.

The mental algebra that Donders proposed is sometimes referred to as subtractive logic. The reasoning is very similar to that used by Helmholtz. It goes like this.

The 'a' (simple) reaction just requires the determination that the signal has occurred as a condition for releasing a previously prepared response. No choice between different alternative responses is necessary. The 'b' (choice) reaction requires all that is entailed by the 'a' reaction but, in addition, the processes of discrimination (of the stimulus) and choice (of the response). The 'c' reaction resembles the 'b' reaction in requiring stimulus discrimination, and is like the 'a' reaction in that if a response is made it is one that has been prepared in advance, and thus only needs to be released.

Given this analysis of the three types of reaction the same subtractive logic as was used by Helmholtz leads to the following equations defining the time occupied by the processes of discrimination and choice:

Discrimination time = 'c' − 'a'
Choice time   = 'b' − 'c'

In 1879 the world's first psychological laboratory was established by Wundt in Leipzig. It was devoted to a number of empirical techniques and the reaction time method dominated these. One of the objectives of the laboratory was to explore Donders' proposals.

Quite soon it became apparent that the 'c' reaction was not equivalent to the 'a' reaction in lacking a choice component. The subject had to choose whether to respond or not. In order to counter this criticism Wundt himself designed a new reaction – the 'd' reaction.

In the 'd' reaction subjects received the same stimulus presentation as in the 'b' reaction. However, they were instructed to respond with a common response as soon as they detected the

24

stimulus and had determined its exact nature. Having made the common response (which thus involved no choice amongst responses) they were then to *tell* the experimenter which stimulus had actually been presented.

This reaction in turn ran into difficulties. They were twofold. First, the empirical difficulty was that highly practised subjects produced 'd' RTs (reaction times) which were as fast as 'a' RTs. Following Donders' logic this implied that discrimination occupied no time at all. The logical difficulty was that subjects reported in their introspections that their preparation for the different types of reaction was not the same, Donders' reasoning depends upon the assumption that the 'c' (or, according to Wundt, the 'd') reaction is simply the 'a' reaction with 'discrimination' *inserted* and so on.

It is clear that the 'd' reaction is not methodologically sound. There is nothing to prevent the subject from responding as soon as he detects any stimulus and then, at his leisure, working out which one it actually was. If this happened the recorded RT would not contain an element attributable to stimulus discrimination and one might very well expect the 'd' reaction to have the same latencies as the 'a' reaction to which it logically reduces. In effect, the experimenter using the 'd' reaction loses control of the experimental situation, a step that is seldom to be encouraged! (See A8.)

As we have seen, one of the principal assumptions underlying Donders' subtractive logic is that the processes responsible for choice reaction performance act sequentially. The input information has to be processed serially through a number of stages. At least in theory quite different information processing schemes can be envisaged. For example, the choice stage might overlap in time with the operation of the discrimination stage, or, more radically, the kind of processing underlying the 'b' reaction might be qualitatively quite different from that which occurs during the 'a', 'c' or 'd' reactions. Uncertainty about the actual nature of these processes and their operation inhibited further development of this methodology until quite recently.

Recent developments on stages in formation processing
The assumption of non-overlapping serial stages in information processing was crucial to Donders' reasoning. It has recently been given convincing support by a series of experiments reported by Sternberg (1969, 1975). While these experiments

use a paradigm that is an extension of the choice reaction time experiment described above they show how, with ingenuity, the apparently unknowable features of hypothesized underlying mechanisms can be revealed.

The essential feature of Sternberg's experimental paradigm is to present to the subject a set of different stimuli and then another stimulus. The subject is required to respond 'yes' or 'no' depending upon whether he thinks the finally presented (test) stimulus was or was not a member of the previously presented (target) set. This paradigm is often called 'memory scanning' since, in principle, the subject has to scan his memory and com-

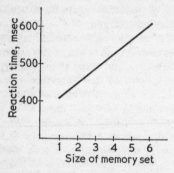

Fig. 2.1 *Graph showing typical relation between reaction time (RT) and the size of the memory (target) set in a memory-scanning experiment. Positive (yes) and negative (no) responses yield identical average RTs.*

pare the test stimulus with his memory of those in the target set. The main dependent (recorded) variable is the latency of his decision response. One of the most common elaborations of this experiment is to vary the number of items in the target set, thereby changing the number of implicit comparisons that have to be made before the subject can respond either positively (yes) or negatively (no). In this way data can be obtained to produce a graph of the latency functions like that shown in Figure 2.1.

There are several striking regularities in the data obtained in these experiments. First is the constancy of search times. The linear increasing latency functions show that each additional member of the target set prolongs the search by a constant amount, between 35 and 40 milliseconds. Sternberg interprets

26

this to mean that the search amongst the items in the memory set proceeds serially. That is, each item is compared in turn with the test item. These linear slopes are found when various kinds of material are used, and for subjects as different as children, college students, schizophrenics and alcoholics. In fact, the slope is related to the nature of the material so that the scanning rate (time per item in the target set) is most rapid for digits and slowest for nonsense syllables, with letters, words and geometric shapes lying in between. It is also remarkable that practice does not seem to alter the scanning rate.

Though the *slopes* of these latency functions are often stable, other features of them may alter. The principal changes are in the general level of the function indicated quantitatively by the intercept on the vertical axis of the graph. Thus schizophrenics are found to have a larger intercept (generally respond more slowly) than alcoholics, who are in turn slower than 'normals'. Practice produces a systematic improvement in performance as shown by a decrease in the intercept of the latency functions, although their slopes remain unchanged.

The second impressive regularity is that almost invariably the slopes of the latency functions for positive and negative responses are identical. That is, it takes as long to decide that a stimulus *was* present in the array as it does to decide that it was *not*. The simplest explanation of this is that the search amongst the memory set is an *exhaustive* one and is not terminated as soon as a match is found between the test item and one in the target set. The extraordinary aspect of this view (as Sternberg readily acknowledges) is that the search goes on even after a match in the target set has been found. If the search procedure were *self-terminating* when a match was achieved, it would be expected that the negative latency function would have a slope that was twice as steep as the positive. This follows because it would take, on average, twice as long to search the whole set than half the set, and if the item was present it would be found, on average, after half the set had been searched.

A final point that has important consequences for generalizing the results obtained using this paradigm to other situations is that the basic features of the results are not altered by using the same target set on every trial and just changing the test stimulus. It is therefore reasonable to conclude that this is a general feature of the way we search through memory lists.

The reason for introducing the Sternberg paradigm in this

book as well as in *Perception and Information* (A4) is not so much because it is of direct consequence for understanding skill, but because it exemplifies a particular methodology for separating out the principal underlying mechanisms. The argument is straightforward. If two independent variables applied together have effects which are simply predictable by adding the effects they have when applied separately, they are said to act additively. If their joint effect is not a simple addition of their separate effects they are said to interact. If two variables are found to have additive effects on response latencies, it is inferred that they affect different processing stages. Likewise, if they interact with each other, they both act on the same stage. For example, the legibility of the test stimulus and the size of the memory set both affect response latency, but they do so additively. The effect of

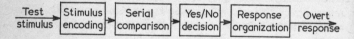

Fig. 2.2 *Diagram showing four hypothetical stages of processing in a memory-scanning experiment. The four stages are influenced selectively by stimulus legibility, the size of the memory set, the type of response and the relative frequency of the response, respectively* (after Steinberg, 1975).

memory set size is not dependent upon the degree of legibility of the test stimulus. It is inferred therefore that these variables act on different processing stages (Sternberg, 1969). By investigating the additivity of effect of several pairs of independent variables, a pattern can be built up which provides a basis for inferring the existence of particular, serially organized stages.

In Figure 2.2 are shown four stages which are designed to act in sequence. These stages have been conceived of to account for performance in item recognition experiments based on the memory scanning paradigm. For example, four independent variables, stimulus legibility, the size of the target set, the type of response and the relative frequency of each type of response, all affect performance but they do so in an additive fashion. In this way Sternberg has effectively established the existence of non-overlapping stages of information processing which are essentially an elaboration of those postulated by Donders a century earlier. Some of these stages are also components of the model outlined in Chapter 1.

Perhaps the most striking phenomenon in the reaction time literature is the way in which reaction time increases as the number of stimuli that may be presented and the number of responses from which to choose are increased. This effect was reported by Merkel (1885) but it was not until sixty-five years later that its implications were begun to be explored. These explorations gave rise to a general relation between reaction time and degree of choice which is called Hick's Law, after Hick's seminal paper, published in 1952.

This article was to become one of the most influential of its kind. It appeared at a time when psychology was just beginning to grasp the significance of information theory. This was a system of measurement devised to quantify communications systems from radio-telephony to computers. In the early 1950s a large number of psychologists 'discovered' Shannon's (1949) definitive work on information theory (also known as communication theory) and sought to apply it to behavioural instead of engineering systems. It was the beginning of the general information-processing approach to psychology which has since dominated considerations of the basic processes underlying behaviour.

Before proceeding to discuss Hick's Law it is necessary to give in outline the essentials of information theory in order that his contributions may be better appreciated. As theories get more sophisticated, increasingly rigorous tests have to be found. The more exactly specified a theory the more precise the predictions are that can be made from it. Mathematical formulations make it easier to derive predictions and so to determine situations in which to test the theory. Furthermore, such precise formulations also allow some quantitative predictions to be made about behaviour. Information theory has provided one basis for making quantitative predictions in psychology.

Information theory

Perhaps the single most confusing aspect of information theory is that it is about 'how much' *not* 'what'. It is therefore a metric or system of measurement, not a theory of semantics or meaning. The second, and the distinguishing, feature of the theory which tends to confuse is that it stresses the events that *might* have happened in addition to that one which actually did.

Consider the statement 'It is raining here today'. The sportsman might be interested in this because it would perhaps make his visit to a cricket match pointless, but increase his catch if he were a fisherman. He is responding to the implications of the message. In contrast, the information theorist is not concerned with implication, only with the extent to which the message has reduced uncertainty. In fact, there is a direct relation between information and uncertainty reduction. The theory quite simply attaches to a *particular* event an amount of information which is related directly to the likelihood (or rather the unlikelihood) of that event. If the 'rain today' message comes from Crete in July (when it hardly ever rains) it conveys a lot of information because it describes a very unlikely state of affairs. This message from a town in the monsoon season conveys hardly any information at all. The same concept leads to newspapers devoting more space to a 'man bites dog' story than to the more likely 'dog bites man'.

However, information theory is seldom applied to single messages. Instead it is used to quantify the *average* amount of information conveyed by *all possible messages* stemming from the same source. This average has, of course, to be weighted by taking into account the relative frequency of the different messages. 'Dry today' messages will occur more often than 'rain today' messages from Crete in July. The equation which defines this average amount of information is:

$$H = \Sigma p_i \log_2 1/P_i$$

where P_i is the probability (or likelihood) of a particular message, i. The Greek capital letter Σ (called sigma) is a symbol used to indicate that the term it governs should be evaluated for each value of i and the sum calculated.

This equation shows that *average* information depends upon the likelihoods of all the messages that *might* occur. It is not so obvious that this average is highest if the different possible messages are equally likely. Thus the average information in weather messages from Margate in August will be higher than in those from Crete. This is because the weather in Margate is more uncertain and all messages about its weather convey about the same amount of information. Because it is nearly always dry in Crete, individual weather messages conveying a lot of information, that is reports of rain, occur only rarely and the resulting *average* amount of information is low.

The basic information theory equation shown above reduces to a simpler form when the alternatives are equiprobable. That is, average amount of information,

$$H = \log_2 n$$

where n is the number of such equiprobable alternatives. In this form of the equation it is clear that as the number of alternative messages increases so does the *average* amount of information they convey.

In summary, then, messages drawn from a large set of possible messages convey more information than those drawn from a small set, and equally likely messages convey more information than do messages when one is more likely than the others. Essentially, the amount of information conveyed is equal to the amount of uncertainty reduced and the greatest prior uncertainty is when there are many *possible* messages all as likely as each other.

The effect of the logarithmic transformation deserves a brief comment. First it should be noted that the base of the logarithm is a fairly unusual one, namely 2. Logarithms to base 10 (common logarithms) or to base e (natural or Naperian logarithms) are more familiar. However, one use of this theory is in quantifying the performance of inorganic communication channels, including computers which operate on a binary, two-state, logic. In that context binary (base 2) logarithms would appear naturally to commend themselves. Generalizing that application to behaviour is less obvious, and may eventually turn out to be of little point. However some practical justification lies in the fact that information conveyed by neurons in the form of all-or-nothing action potentials is also encoded in a binary form. It may be some consolation to note that the base of the logarithms is conventional but not critical. Use of common logarithms (base 10) will alter the size of the units of information so calculated but will not alter the fundamental relations of the theory.

If logarithms to base 2 are used the unit of information defined by the above equations is the BIT, which is a name derived as a contraction of Binary DigIT. The reader may contemplate what name would have been chosen for a unit based on logarithms to base nine.

This new form of measurement has been applied comprehensively to behavioural situations with varying degrees of

31

success. One of the more fruitful of these applications has been to choice reaction time tasks.

Reaction times and amount of information processed
Merkel (1885) found that in a choice reaction time task, response latency increased as the extent of choice increased. However, he found that this relation was a complex one. The slope of the function decreased as the number of alternative choices increased, approaching but never reaching a horizontal line (see Fig. 2.3). This was for different numbers of choices up to ten. Hick (1952) did an experiment which confirmed this general picture. An earlier examination of Merkel's data suggested that a complex curved relation might be replaced by a much more convenient straight line if latency was plotted against the logarithm of the number of choices, that is, log n. As we have seen

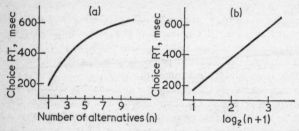

Fig. 2.3 (a) *Curvilinear relation between choice reaction time (RT) and the number of alternatives* (after Merkel, 1885). (b) *Linear relation between choice RT and* $\log_2 (n+1)$ *where n is the number of alternatives. This relation is Hick's Law* (after Hick, 1952).

this quantity has a special significance in information theory: it is the information conveyed by messages about n equiprobable alternative events. In a nutshell, it looked as if response latency might be accounted for in terms of the amount of information the subject had to process. If this were so it would go a long way towards establishing amount of information as a psychological variable.

In fact a close scrutiny of his data indicated to Hick that the best straight line fit was obtained by plotting response latency not against *log n* but against *log (n + 1)*. This relation is shown in Figure 2.3. The amendment requires comment. In his experiment subjects had to press keys depending upon which of several lights was lit. In advance of the stimulus appearing, subjects were uncertain both about which light would come on and about when it would do so. The $+1$ in Hick's equation makes explicit allowance for that temporal uncertainty. In experiments in which subjects present themselves with the stimuli, thereby removing temporal uncertainty, the $+1$ is an unnecessary addition to the basic equation. This is true for card-sorting (Crossman, 1953).

Although Hick explored the case where the alternatives were equiprobable, it was Hyman (1953) who obtained evidence for the general application of information theory to the choice reaction time situation. The theory stipulates that there are three ways in which amount of information, H, may be changed. Altering the number of equiprobable events is one of these. In addition, H is also altered by manipulating the *relative frequency* of the events and by changing the extent to which knowledge of the previous event delimits the likelihood of the next event, that is its *sequential dependency*. For example, in English the letter 'q' is always followed by the letter 'u', so given a 'q' the next letter is perfectly predictable and its occurrence conveys no information at all.

Hyman varied all three factors in a choice reaction time experiment that effectively established the information theory index as a fundamental predictor of average reaction time. This general relation is called the Hick-Hyman Law.

Transmitted information. The calculation of H described above is determined wholly by the distribution of probabilities of messages of different kinds. At best it specifies quantitatively the problem facing the subject, that is the information load presented to him. By relating reaction time to this quantity it is implicitly assumed that he actually transmits (processes) all of that information and, therefore, that H represents the mental work he is doing. However, it is rare for subjects, when instructed to respond as quickly as possible, to make no errors at all. Typically error rates are between 1 and 5 per cent. One might wonder what effect errors would have since they presumably occur because the subject has not processed the information presented to him on that trial. There is a relatively straightforward extension of the calculations described above that permits an adjustment to be made for inconsistencies in

33

the subject's behaviour. If the subject always makes the same response exclusively to the same stimulus (but regardless of whether he actually obeys the instructions he was given!) he will transmit all the input (presented) information. The more inconsistencies that occur in his performance the lower the value of transmitted information. Ultimately if he performs completely randomly he will be transmitting no information at all.

The calculation of transmitted information has to be done after the event, since there is no way of predicting subjects' errors (inconsistencies) in advance. However, transmitted information takes error rate into account and therefore automatically accommodates the trade-off between speed and accuracy, which is a feature of performance. It is encouraging to discover that transmitted information continues to provide a sound predictor of reaction time even when the error-rate is as high as 10 per cent.

Stimulus discrimination versus response selection
We shall deal with the Hick-Hyman Law more fully in the next chapter. Here we shall consider one particular interpretation.

The data seem to indicate that reaction time is a linear increasing function of the amount of information transmitted by the subject in his choosing behaviour. On the assumption that he works at a constant rate, transmitted information may be treated as a measure of mental work accomplished and the slope of the reaction time function represents his speed of working. If he works very fast a relatively flat function should be observed, indicating that each unit of mental work has added a relatively small increment in processing time. If he processes information slowly a steeper function would be expected. The question is then raised as to what sort of mental work is being performed. Referring back to Donders' original analysis (see p. 24), the two most obvious processes are stimulus discrimination and response selection.

Although there is some controversy regarding the relative contributions of these two processes Morin and Forrin (1963) have attempted to resolve the issue by manipulating the mapping ratio in reaction time experiments. The mapping ratio is the ratio of the number of stimuli to the number of responses. If there is a different response for each stimulus there is a one-to-one mapping ratio. However, experiments may be contrived in which several different stimuli are mapped onto the same response and vice versa. In these many-to-one and one-to-many mapping arrangements stimulus uncertainty and response uncertainty may be separately manipulated. It is then possible to ascertain their relative effects. Using this technique it seems that both sources of uncertainty influence performance. More importantly it is found that response uncertainty (and therefore the process of response selection) is about twice as important as stimulus uncertainty (stimulus discrimination) in determining reaction time.

It will be recalled that the Sternberg paradigm (see p. 26) gives rise to a linear relation between reaction time and the size of the memory (target) set. This contrasts with the logarithmic relation between reaction time and the number of alternative stimuli (and responses) which is Hick's Law. Some reconciliation between these results is necessary. The situation is made more complex by Briggs' (1974) report of an analysis of 145 studies utilizing the Sternberg paradigm and the discovery that 62 per cent of them reported data that were fitted better by a logarithmic function than the linear function claimed by Sternberg.

There are two main points to make. First, the data examined by Briggs are fitted very well by both linear and logarithmic functions in most instances. The problem is that with very few points spanning a small range, discovering non-linearity is extremely difficult. The nature of the Sternberg paradigm tends to encourage the use of small target sets seldom exceeding four items. Secondly, the degree of curvature in memory scanning data seems appreciably less than that typical of choice reaction time data.

Sternberg postulates a number of non-overlapping sequential stages in information processing. The matching of the test item with the members of the target set is considered to occur early in this sequence (cf. Fig. 2.2), and two stages before the selection of a response. In the Sternberg paradigm every trial is a two-choice task in terms of choosing a response. If the size of the target set is changed, however, this alters the number of stimuli and so affects the mapping-ratio. For example, with a set size of two (and, of course, two responses) the ratio is one-to-one, but with a set size of four the ratio will be two-to-one.

There is then no essential conflict between the functions revealed by the two paradigms, if one interprets the results of choice reaction time experiments as manifesting a mixture of effects. Increasing the number of alternative stimuli will produce a linear (or near linear) effect on reaction time in the same way as increasing the target (memory) set size affects latency in the Sternberg paradigm. However, increasing the number of response alternatives, which in a one-to-one mapping is an inevitable concomitant of increasing the number of alternative stimuli, alters the load on the response selection stage and thereby produces a logarithmic effect on reaction time. The evidence suggests that the effect on the response selection stage predominates.

In summary, it is congruent with data to propose that separate stages determine the nature of incoming stimuli and decide upon the response to be executed. The former stage takes an amount of time which is a simple linear function of the number of alternatives and thus implies that the process involves a serially organized scan of those alternatives. In contrast, response selection time is related to the information load imposed by the degree of choice. This is indicated by the fact that as choice expands choice time increases logarithmically. However, as we shall see later, though information theory offers a means of describing and integrating experimental data in terms of the system of measurement it provides, it does not necessarily reveal the *nature* of the process which gives rise to the logarithmic function.

3
A matter of choice

Information theory
By the mid-1950s information theory had been established as the most fruitful basis for an explanation of how choice reaction times are lengthened as the extent of choice increases; by the end of that decade it was clear that information theory was not going to provide the whole story. This appreciation of its limited usefulness stemmed from two sources. First, data were obtained that indicated that some factors affected reaction time but did not fit nicely into an informational context. Secondly, it became clear that information theory did not necessarily offer a satisfactory account of the operation of underlying mechanisms even if it did describe their overall performance in general terms.

Contrary data
One could say that 1959 was a very bad year for information theory. Two papers appeared that year which still defy a satisfactory explanation. Leonard reported an experiment which appeared to show that provided the relation between stimulus and response was exceptionally close, choice reaction time was independent of extent of choice. Almost simultaneously Mowbray and Rhoades showed that after a collossal amount of practice, extending over three months, on a task involving pressing keys selectively to light stimuli, the usual difference between four-choice and two-choice RT disappeared.

Leonard's experiment is almost unique in the literature. He

had his subjects rest their finger-tips on vibrators and they were instructed to press down with whichever finger was stimulated by its vibrator. With only a limited amount of practice (comparable with the majority of experiments in this field) he found a consistent difference between simple and choice reaction time but no difference between two-choice and eight-choice reaction times. The usual logarithmic relation of Hick and Hyman was absent.

This finding is important for two reasons. First it establishes that a factor can operate to obscure the usual effect. Secondly, the implications of a horizontal latency function are potentially very serious. We saw in the last chapter how the slope of the latency function could be interpreted as an index of the rate of information processing, the flatter the slope the higher the rate. In many manual reaction times a rate of about five bits per second is observed. A horizontal latency function such as Leonard reported would correspond to an infinitely high rate of information processing. Such a rate is inconceivable in a limited system and so is puzzling.

Mowbray and Rhoades' experiment, though it poses a similar problem, took a quite different form. They experimented intensively on a single subject who was hired by them for the whole of one summer. During this time he performed tens of thousands of reaction time responses and can be considered to have been very highly practised indeed. At the beginning of this series the usual relation between simple, two-choice and four-choice reaction times were observed. After three months of concentrated practice only the difference between simple and choice reaction time remained. In this sense the data resembled those from Leonard's subjects, and much the same problems are posed by them. Perhaps the major difference is that whereas Leonard used a task involving an unusually close connection between stimulus and response, Mowbray and Rhoades' task was unexceptional; only the length of practice (and hence, perhaps, the level of skill) was out of the ordinary.

Stimulus-response (S-R) compatibility
Some years earlier Fitts and Seeger (1953) had postulated a variable which they called stimulus-response compatibility, to account for a number of effects on performance that seemed to be due not to the stimuli or the responses in a direct way, but rather to the particular *combination* of stimulus and response

that was used in the experiment. The concept of S-R compatibility is not usually very difficult to communicate, being essentially a measure of the extent to which the instructed response is a 'natural' one to make to the particular stimulus (see E4). For example, in a piece of apparatus comprising two stimulus lights and two response keys, it is more 'natural', and hence compatible, to press the right-hand key to the right-hand light than to the left-hand light. Compatibility is related, in that case, to spatial relation. However, it is a different matter when it comes to trying to produce an operational definition of S-R compatibility which, all too often, reverts to some kind of intuitive judgement. In consequence, the degree of compatibility of a particular S-R arrangement cannot be calculated objectively and one tends to fall back on the postulated effects of degree of compatibility as an index. Unfortunately, that is the entry to a circular argument with a disconcertingly small radius. Fast reaction times are due to high S-R compatibility which is indicated by the fast reaction times! However, even in the absence of an independent means of assessing degree of compatibility, the concept seems plausible and worth pursuing. The future may provide the techniques for independent quantitative assessment.

One application of the compatibility concept is to argue that when there is very high S-R compatibility the 'normal' processes for choosing responses are unnecessary and, instead, the response is made as a result of the activation of an almost direct connection between stimulus and response. This mode of operation sounds a bit like a telephone exchange with sundry connections between particular inputs and outputs. If this were the case it would be inappropriate to interpret the latency function as a measure of information processing since the mode of processing is different, and, in a sense, responding is 'automatic'.

If this view is considered in relation to Mowbray and Rhoades' data, it follows that the effect of massively prolonged practice is greatly to increase the compatibility of the S-R relations defined in their experiment. In Britain light switches go down for on, but in the USA they go up. Both relations seem 'natural' to the respective populations. This clearly has considerable implications for real-life situations in which many initially strange and awkward combinations of stimulus and response become, over years of continued practice, familiar and natural. For example, consider driving a car.

Fitts and Posner (1967) summarize a number of studies which report various slopes of the latency function (see Fig. 3.1). The steepest slopes are associated with tasks which involved pressing keys to numbers or coding a particular light as a numeral. Somewhat flatter slopes were found for tasks in which the key to be pressed was spatially related to the light that was lit, and flatter still where subjects simply had to say which of several digits was presented. In general, the closer the

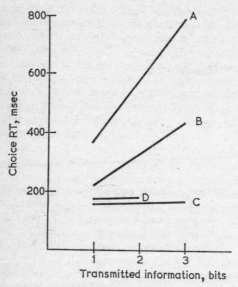

Fig. 3.1 *Schematic representation of various relations between choice reaction time (RT) and amount of transmitted information (this takes errors into account), obtained under four conditions:*

A – pressing numbered keys to displayed digits
B – pressing keys as indicated by lights above them
C – pressing down with whichever finger was stimulated with a vibrator
D – as for B but after about 50,000 trials.

The variation in the slopes of these RT functions is sometimes attributed to variation in stimulus-response compatibility (after Fitts and Posner, 1967).

spatial correspondence between stimulus and response or the more direct the relation between them, the flatter the latency function.

The logarithmic latency function and underlying processes

The status of information theory as an *explanation* of choice reaction-time functions is less clear than is its basis as a *description*. There are two principal alternative interpretations. First, the critical features which determine performance are the informational load of the task and the system's information-processing capacity. Secondly, the underlying processes are not governed by informational principles but the overall performance of the system just happens to mirror, in general terms, the information theory relation. Let us consider these possibilities.

The information-processing capacity hypothesis essentially demands that the human subject takes longer to solve more difficult problems, difficulty being determined by the metric of information theory. As shown above, information-processing rate is then indicated by the slope of the latency function and for a particular task this appears a feasible hypothesis, at least for tasks where the range of choice does not exceed ten alternatives. However, the discovery that different tasks are characterized by different slopes, depending, apparently, upon degrees of S-R compatibility, complicates that idea. It would seem necessary to assume either that the information-processing capacity of the system changes with the task or that the informational loading of a task is determined by its S-R compatibility. The latter is the more plausible, but little progress has been made towards a quantitative specification of this effect.

Serial dichotomization

Some attempt has to be made to explain how the informational relation in the latency function might arise. A suggestion that stems more or less directly from information theory was explored by Hick (1952) and Welford (1968). It is that the selection process has to isolate one particular response from amongst the possible alternatives. One efficient way of achieving this end is to make a series of decisions, reducing the set of alternatives by half on each decision. Thus two alternatives would require one decision, four need two, eight need three and so on. If each component decision takes a constant time,

41

response latency would be a linear function of the number of decisions, or, equivalently, a logarithmic function of the number of alternatives.

This conceptualization of the operation of the underlying processes is attractive when the number of alternatives is a power of two and the alternatives are equiprobable. It is more difficult, however, to apply it to cases where some alternatives are more probable than others or when the number of alternatives takes on awkward values, like seven, which are not a power of two. One possible way round this difficulty is to assume that the selection process divides the set remaining at each decision into two subsets of equal aggregate probability. So in an example where one response is four times more likely than each of the other four, the first decision would be to contrast the likely alternative against the rest considered as a block. This would result in early detection of the likely alternative, if it occurred, and slower detection of the less likely alternatives. This general relation mirrors observed data.

Problems with serial dichotomization
There are, however, a number of difficulties with this scheme which are not so easily resolved. The first of these concerns the specification of a process that can determine that a particular event is contained in a subset of events but cannot identify which particular member of that subset matches with it. The example often used to exemplify the successive decision principle is to consider the identification of a counterfeit coin amongst a set of, say, eight. Suppose the counterfeit coin weighs slightly less than the genuine article. It is then possible to identify the subset of coins containing the dud by balancing it against another subset containing an equal number of genuine coins. The initial set of eight may be divided into two sets of four which are placed on the opposing scale-pans of a balance. The pan which rises is the one containing the counterfeit coin. That subset of four is now divided into two subsets of two, and so on until eventually a single coin is balanced against one other and found to be lighter. The problem has then been solved. In this example three weighings would be required.

This dud-detection problem exemplifies the principle but its persuasive power depends upon the particular properties of coins and the fact that the problem is to detect the single maverick in an otherwise homogeneous set. It is very much more difficult to imagine how a comparable system would work if the problem were uniquely to define one out of a set of heterogeneous alternatives differing one from another along a number of dimensions.

A further difficulty surrounds giving an account of the effects of frequency imbalance. In a two-choice task there has to be exactly one dichotomous comparison no matter how great the imbalance of probability between the two alternatives. That leaves rather little opportunity for such imbalance to be reflected in the response latencies.

The final difficulty with the serial dichotomizing scheme is that, as Hick pointed out in 1952, it predicts that reaction times should be least variable for those situations which logically require a whole number of sub-decisions, for example two, four or eight alternative choices and so on. When the number of alternatives is not a power of two, several choices from the same set of alternatives may involve different numbers of decisions and so more variable response times should be observed. They are not. Reaction time variability (variance) tends to increase steadily as the number of alternatives from which to choose goes up.

Alternative schemes

One alternative to the serial dichotomous elimination scheme, which incorporates a series of sub-decisions, is to consider a procedure which involves replicating the target response so that sufficient versions exist to allow comparisons with each of the alternatives to be made simultaneously. Suppose the replication process could be a reproductive function such that each replicate can give rise to two identical versions of itself and the time for each replicative process is constant. In this case the time to produce as many replicates as there are alternatives will be, approximately, a logarithmic function of the number of alternatives. This scheme avoids the first of the difficulties of the serial dichotomization procedure outlined above, but shares the difficulties it has with accounting for frequency imbalance effects. Perhaps a radically different sort of approach is required.

Smith (1968) examined a number of theories that had set out to give an account of the processes underlying choice reaction latencies. He concluded first that none of the extant theories provided a satisfactory account of the phenomena and, secondly, that theorists had concentrated on the stimulus discrimination stage (see Ch. 2). It now seems clear that though stimulus discrimination has some effect on response latencies in two-choice tasks, the effects of changing the number of response alternatives and their relative frequency are the more important determinants of the Hick-Hyman Law. In short, it is to the response selection processes that we should look if an understanding of that law is to be found.

Some hints are offered by the phenomenon of the repetition effect. If a stimulus is repeated on successive trials the reaction time to it is substantially reduced. Closer examination reveals that this advantage is, in part, dependent upon subjects correctly predicting the repetition (Whitman and Geller, 1972). Observing a subject carrying out a card-sorting task shows much the same thing quite clearly. He tends to hold the face-down pack of cards nearer to one pile than the others and may even make an initial movement towards it which may have to be corrected.

Theios and Falmagne (1971) and Theios *et al.* (1973) have described a model which may be developed to account for these phenomena. Essentially it consists of an ordered stack of implicit responses which are reordered after each trial, the last required response being moved to the top of the stack. It is then proposed that response selection depends simply on a linear self-terminating search of this stack. It is clear that frequently required responses will be 'found' quicker than those rarely required and repetition effects are obviously accommodated. Whether it will prove sufficient in other ways as well is yet to be determined. It is clear that compatibility phenomena would require additional theoretical assumptions for their explanation, but, as yet, no model has appeared that offers an integrated explanation of choice reaction data in general.

The generality of the logarithmic latency function

Much of this chapter has been devoted to a discussion of the Hick-Hyman Law which asserts a logarithmic latency function for choice reaction time. It is a replicable relation and it has teased researchers for nearly a quarter of a century. However, it is certainly not the only function of interest in this area and, in terms of the real world, it may not even be the most important. There are three situations to contrast with the moderate degree of compatibility, moderate level of practice and few alternatives which characterize the laboratory experiments on reaction time that give credence to the Hick-Hyman Law.

The first of these we have already met. It is the over-trained subject in Mowbray and Rhoades' experiment who reportedly produced the same response latency in two- and four-choice tasks after extended practice. In everyday life there are many circumstances in which people are highly trained in making choices amongst a limited number of well-defined alternatives. If this behaviour is part of their work it is likely that they will become massively over-practised, quite soon after entering that occupation. Mowbray and Rhoades' subject may be far from unique.

The second situation lies at the other extreme. It is exemplified in an experiment reported by Kirkby (1974). He used specially constructed cards (not ordinary playing cards) in a card-sorting task, in other respects similar to Crossman's (1953). Crossman reported results that gave an excellent fit to the Hick-Hyman Law, that is a logarithmic latency function. However, Kirkby required his subjects to sort the cards into locations that were randomly rather than systematically chosen. He found that the data were very well described by a straight-line function relating choice time to the number of equiprobable categories. The key to this discrepancy would appear to be the relative unfamiliarity of the subjects with *where* each category of card had to be put. Or to put it another way, the translation rule which defined the required object modulation (see p. 17) was operating relatively inefficiently so the subject had to re-establish the rule on most trials. The point we are making here is that when the level of practice is relatively low, the logarithmic function does not appear. It seems to be dependent upon sufficient practice establishing rapid and accurate access to the translation rule which defines the required object modulation, but not too much practice because that may cause the latency function virtually to disappear altogether.

The third and final instance of a serious deviation from the Hick-Hyman Law is associated with using a large number of alternatives. Seibel (1963) reported an experiment in which subjects were required to select amongst 1023 different responses. These were defined by considering all possible combinations of key-presses by the ten fingers and thumbs. For most of these the subjects had to play chords. A considerable amount of practice was given so it cannot be argued that subjects were performing while still unfamiliar with the task. The relation between reaction time and number of alternatives is depicted in Figure 3.2. This shows that up to between sixteen and twenty alternatives the logarithmic curve of the Hick-Hyman Law is found, but further increases in the number of alternatives have little effect on reaction time. It is also clear that variability of

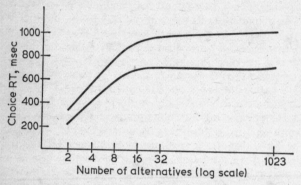

Fig. 3.2 *Graph showing schematically the relation between choice reaction time (RT) and number of alternatives. The lines indicate the range of RTs found for different numbers of alternatives. Up to about twelve alternatives the function follows the Hick-Hyman Law. With a further increase in the number of alternatives performance becomes more variable but there is hardly any increase in the average RT. Performance was measured after several thousand practice trials* (after Seibel, 1963).

performance is appreciably higher for that part of the curve which is near enough horizontal.

Though this latter example of a breakdown of the Hick-Hyman function might not have been expected, on reflection it was almost inevitable.

Response generation instead of response selection

We have been assuming that choice reaction time data stem from the operation of a system that chooses from amongst a limited set of alternative responses. This set is apparently defined by the responses which may be required in the experiment. It would be efficient to limit the system in this way rather than waste time searching through a welter of irrelevant responses. However, it is self-evident that there must be a limit to the number of responses that can be held in a repertoire, if only because the brain has a limited size.

It is equally obvious that there must be some way for the system to make a response other than by selecting from a pre-prepared set of implicit responses. Otherwise a novel response would be impossible and the adult would be no more skilful than the infant. To distinguish this alternative to response selection we will call it response generation. Responses that are generated as opposed to selected are somehow assembled from more primitive elements to satisfy some current demand defined, in the model, by the required object modulation.

Two things follow from this hypothesis. First, responses of a given order of complexity should take about the same amount of time to prepare from primitive elements. Secondly, there must be some break-even point when response selection takes as long as response generation. It then follows that if the number of alternatives is increased beyond this critical number it will be quicker to design a response from scratch than to search through a large number of pre-prepared alternatives.

4
Making movements

So far we have given some consideration to how responses are chosen on the assumption that once chosen the response will be executed. It is now necessary to examine more closely the processes involved in assembling responses and in their execution. It was argued in Chapter 1 that the most revealing sorts of tasks for this kind of study are those which prohibit a correction being superimposed upon the initial response. The kinds of tasks which do this best are discrete aiming tasks. These are tasks which require subjects to make responses towards targets which by their size determine the tolerance of inaccuracy that is acceptable. In Chapter 1 we noted a number of real-life contest situations which involve such tasks.

The accuracy of rapid movements

One of the most important observations about aiming performance was made by Woodworth (1899). He showed that if a subject is encouraged to make responses so that they are completed in a specified length of time, the quicker the response the less accurate it is. However, the more startling finding was that responses which were made very quickly indeed were just as accurate when the subject closed his eyes! It is worth elaborating the experiment a little more, if only better to admire the contrast between the simplicity of the method and the significance of the results. The basic task was one in which subjects had to draw a series of lines, each beneath the last and so on. Each line had to be the same length. The line-drawing rate was paced with a metronome and the dependent variable was how accurately each line approximated the initial example. The fastest rates set on the metronome would have required subjects to draw about three lines each second. A further factor in the experiment was whether or not subjects were allowed to view their performance.

It was not at all surprising that when the lines were drawn relatively slowly, so that about a second could be spent on each response, there was a massive difference between the 'seeing' and 'blindfold' performance. As the response rate was increased, so that a correspondingly shorter time was available for each movement, accuracy under the 'seeing' condition fell. However, blindfolded accuracy was maintained. The extraordinary result was that for rates of about 120 per minute and higher there was no difference between subjects who were allowed to see what they were doing and those who were not. The inference is that responses which are completed in a very short time do not benefit from visual information about their accuracy. The critical duration of a response before visual control can be effective would appear to be somewhat less than half a second.

This issue was examined using rather more sophisticated apparatus by Keele and Posner (1968). In their experiment, subjects made discrete aiming responses at a target $\frac{1}{4}$ inch in diameter and 6 inches away from the starting point. Subjects were trained to make movements which took particular lengths of time, either 0·15, 0·25, 0·35 or 0·45 seconds. In the main part of the experiment their success in hitting the target was measured as a function of the length of time they spent on the movement. The critical factor in the experiment was that on some trials the lights illuminating the experimental situation were turned off as soon as the subject started his movement. The results correspond generally quite well with those of Woodworth but offer greater precision since in this experiment the actual duration of each movement was measured.

Accuracy in terms of percentage hits on the target was almost identical for the 'lights on' and 'lights off' conditions for the fastest group of movements. This indicates that visual information about the aiming movement was not incorporated in the control of movements completed in just under 200 milliseconds. The next slowest group of movements were supposed to be executed in 250 milliseconds but in fact subjects took about 260 milliseconds on them. When this much time was spent, there was a small but reliable advantage for movements made with the lights on. Keele and Posner concluded that the critical period for the utilization of visual information in controlling the accuracy of responses is somewhere between 190 and 260 milliseconds.

An even more ingenious test of the same problem was devised by Beggs and Howarth (1970). In their task subjects aimed at a vertical target in front of them. In making the aiming movement their hand was made to pass through a photo-electric beam and, as a result, extinguish the lights so that the target disappeared. The results indicate that if the lights were turned out about 290 milliseconds or less before the movement reached the target, accuracy was not much affected by exactly when they were extinguished. In contrast, turning the lights out earlier than 290 ms before striking the target had a considerable effect, and the earlier they went out, the greater the effect. They concluded that the critical time for making a visually based correction to the aiming response was about 290 ms. Why this time is about 70 ms longer than Keele and Posner's estimate of the same quantity is unexplained. However, it may be that such a difference is quite satisfactorily accounted for in terms of individual differences, degrees of practice and the speed with which the room illumination dropped when the light switch was operated. Taking these results altogether, there now seems to be very strong evidence that, in general, responses lasting less than 250 ms are most unlikely to have been corrected on the basis of visual information about their accuracy.

Ballistic responses

The most obvious conclusion to draw from these experimental studies of aiming accuracy is that the coach's insistence that 'you keep your eye on the ball' can be modified. There is no point in keeping your eye on the ball during the last quarter of a second before impact since during that time whatever stroke you are going to make is committed and the last opportunity to amend its accuracy has passed. It is interesting to calculate just what this means in terms of the distance the ball travels in fast ball games. A baseball pitcher throws a ball at about 100 feet per second which means that the *last* correction the batter can make is based on information when the ball is still 25 feet away from him. This means the ball has travelled only just over half the distance from pitcher to batter. A similar set of figures would apply to a fast bowler in cricket, and only marginally lower speeds would be found in tennis.

In one of the most important theoretical papers in the area (and now regarded as a classic), Craik (1947) characterized the nature of aiming movements as 'ballistic'. By this he meant that such movements are executed without the intervention of centrally computed corrections based upon sensory information about accuracy. Studies of ballistic movements clearly have some special advantages. Since, once under way, they are by definition uncontaminated by correctional changes they provide the clearest, least distorted and most direct means of examining the operation of the response production process.

There are two other points about ballistic movements which are not quite so obvious. First, in operational terms one knows one has a ballistic response when its execution is completed in less than some arbitrary time, say 250 or 300 ms, since these very short-lasting responses are *uncorrectable*. However, the essential concept concerns the *uncorrected* nature of the response, so that responses may well be ballistic even though they last several seconds. The difficulty is to know whether such a temporally extended response is ballistic or not. Secondly there is nothing about the concept of the ballistic response which requires it to be simple. For example, signing one's name could be a ballistic response. So too could changing gear in a car which involves temporally integrated movements of one hand and both feet.

Motor programmes. The major implication of the discovery of ballistic responses is the motor programme. If a response cannot be corrected during the last quarter of a second of its life there must be some internal programme that defines it. Extending the argument as before, the motor programme may very well guide the response for considerably longer than a quarter of a second.

This concept of a motor programme which contains a detailed set of instructions for the operation of coordinated muscular changes throughout the body is the same as the implicit response in the model in Chapter 1. One of the essential problems in seeking to understand the operation of the mechanisms underlying skill is to give an account of the assembly of the implicit response or motor programme. The problem is a particularly difficult one because the mechanism most directly responsible is buried deep in the chain of processing stages. It is difficult either to observe it or to effect some change in its operation

Sensory bases of movement control

In Chapter 1 we began to explore the problems that a man might have in drinking a pint of beer. Just the difficulty of grasping the handle of the tankard proved sufficient to exemplify the mobilization of a host of processes. One of the basic problems then established was the system's need to 'know' about the current state of the effector apparatus so that an appropriate motor programme could be prescribed to solve the problem of reaching the glass.

Using the terms of the model, the task can be translated into the problem of bringing object (hand) and target (glass) into conjunction. In general the object will be influenced by the effectors; in the special case of tankard-grasping they are one and the same. It is evident that one cannot determine how to make the object move to the target unless one knows where the object and target are to begin with.

Locating the object which is at a distance requires a distance sense, and vision is the most precise we have. Although vision cannot accurately locate objects at some considerable distance from an observer (distance becomes increasingly hard to judge as it increases), nearby objects and certainly objects within range for grasping can be located very accurately indeed. This is mainly but not exclusively due to stereoscopic vision. When this is reduced or removed accurate distance perception deteriorates markedly. The next time he is hanging clothes on a clothes-line the reader may note how the line is difficult to pin-point in space. The problem becomes easier if he turns his head on one side as if he were lying down. This change of posture considerably increases stereoscopic cues to the distance of the line and reaching for it becomes a correspondingly less risky business.

In most cases the target is specified visually. If other sensory modalities are to be used instead the target has to have special properties. For example, a version of basket-ball is played by blind sportsmen using a specially constructed ball with a bell inside it. Locating the ball auditorially is now possible, though not with the precision that vision normally allows. The other alternative to visual perception is if the subject can touch the target. Its spatial location can then be inferred from proprioceptive information. Proprioception signals where the parts of the body are with respect to one another. And if you know where your hand is, you also know the location of something your hand is touching.

Determining the location of the object may be a similar problem to localizing the target. In most instances it will be in view so vision can be used. However, rather more often than for the target, it will be either impossible or inconvenient to locate the object visually. These situations are most likely when the object is the effector as it is in catching a ball or grasping a tankard. Returning to our would-be tankard-grasper, he has his hands in his pockets which makes it difficult for him to locate them visually. All he can see is a foreshortened view of the bulge they make. In the case of ball-players one can conceive of catching a ball by first looking at the hand, but it is a matter of fact that catchers do not do it that way, and in any case it would be a potentially catastrophic waste of time to do so.

What alternatives exist to visual localization of the effectors? There are two. One is to use a scheme of 'dead reckoning' as is used in navigation when sight of sun or stars is impossible; the other is to use proprioception.

Dead reckoning. It is possible to calculate where an object is in space if one knows where it was and what has happened to it since. Applying this principle to the problem of localizing the parts of the body, one would need some calibrating observation (possibly visual) to determine a position and then to update this position continuously by taking into account all of the motor commands sent out to muscles which would alter it.

There are two major weaknesses to this scheme. It is implicit that the calculated current position of a limb would have to be based on a series of corrections made for the efferent (motor) signals sent to the muscles. Inevitably it has to be assumed that these signals reached the muscles and had their expected effects. They may not have done so. Secondly, the amount of information processing capacity that would be needed just to keep a running check on where the various bits of one's body are at any moment in time would be astronomical.

It is, however, the case that at least one localization system works in this way. The eyeballs can move quite appreciably in their sockets. One problem that the visual system has is to determine whether a given movement should be attributed to a moving object in the visual field or to a movement of the eyeball and a stationary object. Both situations could give rise to the same relative movement of a visual image on the retina. The brain normally has no difficulty in sorting out this problem. However, it does not do it by observing whether or not the eyeball is rotating. Instead it checks only whether an efferent message has been sent instructing the eyeball to move. This fact has been most convincingly demonstrated using locally applied drugs to paralyse the eye-muscles, thereby immobilizing the eyeball, and then asking the subject to 'look over there' (Gregory, 1966). Trying to carry out this instruction is a nauseating experience. The eyeball, of course, cannot move but the visual world appears to move violently in the direction that the subject 'wills' his eyes to move. What has happened is that the compensatory mechanism, which normally keeps the visual world stable, has corrected for the 'willed' movement of the eyes. However, since the intended movement was never put into effect the compensation was inappropriate and the resulting percept illusory. Had the compensating mechanism any direct information about the state of the eyeballs this effect would not have been observed.

It is difficult to make similar tests on other parts of the body. The eyeballs offer the unique example of an articulated sense organ. However, having found one part of the body that is apparently controlled on the basis of efferent or outflow signals instead of afferent or inflow signals, it is fitting to ask how general the outflow control principle may be. Thus, for example, Jones (1974) strongly favours outflow control as a general principle in the control of active movement (which includes all voluntary movement) relegating proprioception to a minor role in the appreciation of passive movement, and the signalling of local conditions obtaining in muscles and joints. The majority of authors, however, adopt the opposite stance, admitting a small control role for motor outflow, but follow Sherrington (1906) in placing the bulk of the responsibility for 'knowing where one's bits are' on proprioceptive inflow.

On the principle of making use of what is available proprioception would seem to be very well placed to signal the whereabouts of the various parts of the body. There are two main groups of proprioceptors which probably serve this function. They are the joint receptors and the muscle tendon receptors.

Joint receptors

The joint receptors are, as their name suggests, located in the joints. They come in two forms, one which signals the static position (angle) of the joint and one which responds only transiently to static position and thereby provides an indirect but reliable signal about rate of change of joint angle. As with touch receptors in the skin and the coding of sound frequencies in the ear, the actual method of coding joint angle involves a pattern of activity in the joint receptors and so is complex. However, taken together these two kinds of joint receptors, responding to angle and rate of change of angle, are very well placed to signal to the brain the shape of the articulated skeleton (that is the position of each rigid part of it relative to each other part) and also how it is changing in time. At least in theory, and probably in practice also, there is enough information provided by the joint receptor system to allow all the rigid parts of the body to be localized.

It will be appreciated that this kind of perception, like all others, has a large inferential component. The signals from the joints only tell about joint angles, spatial position has to be inferred from them taking into account the length of the rigid parts of the skeleton. In this way the position of a finger-tip relative to the shoulder can be computed from the signalled angles of shoulder, elbow, wrist and finger joints coupled with the known and unchanging lengths of the upper arm, forearm and all other intervening bones. One may wonder how these lengths become known, and how changes during childhood and adolescence are incorporated in the brain's model of its body. The answer to this question turns out to be a complex one (Howard and Templeton, 1966). If it is the mapping of the body perceived visually onto the body perceived proprioceptively that is in question, the bulk of evidence from experiments in which this relation is changed suggests that vision provides the basic reference and proprioception is recalibrated in terms of it.

For example, in experiments in which prisms are placed in front of their eyes, subjects find that this causes their arms to look as if they are in one place while they feel as if they are in another. However, an astonishingly small amount of experience of this new relation between visual and proprioceptive information is sufficient to produce internal changes that bring them back into correspondence. It seems from a number of experiments that the principal change is in the proprioceptive system, vision providing the reference for recalibration.

Tendon receptors
The tendon receptors provide the other aspect of proprioception. They are very small stretch sensitive devices located in the tendons which connect muscles to their anchor points in bones. They signal directly the tension which exists in the tendon which houses them. This information can be interpreted, in the context of the information describing the state of the joint which is affected by the muscle in question, to give a measure of the power being developed in that muscle.

It seems that the tendon receptor system serves a different purpose from the joint receptor system. Whereas the joint receptors can provide information which in some circumstances can take the place of vision, the tendon receptors provide information that cannot be signalled by any other system. It is the tendon receptors which are mainly responsible for our ability to judge the weight of objects we lift. Our estimate depends upon our impression of the force we have to develop in order to stop the object from dropping.

However, weight-lifting is not a particularly vital skill. More important is the role played by the tendon receptors in the determination of the efferent signals which are organized to produce a particular movement. It is an essential feature of muscle control that the same efferent signal will have a different effect depending upon the pre-existing state of the muscle. Therefore if it is desired to produce a particular change in muscle power, the signal mobilized to do this will have to be modified to take account of the current condition of the muscle. It is the tendon receptor system which makes this possible by providing the necessary information.

Motor constancy mechanisms

There are other ways in which movement control is more complicated than it might look on first sight. The important aspect of the response is the torque produced about the joint on which the muscle acts, because it is this torque which actually acts on the outside world. Torque is a measure of twisting power tending to open or close the angle of the joint. The relation between muscle tension and torque is complex. There are two factors to take into account. These are the length of the muscle

(a)   (b)

Fig. 4.1 *Schematic diagram of elbow joint and biceps muscle. Changing the joint angle alters the length of the muscle and its direction of pull on the forearm. The muscle has the best mechanical advantage when it pulls at right angles to the forearm. For this reason the weight that could be supported on the hand in (a) is heavier than that in (b).*

and the angle of the joint. The length of the muscle affects the tension developed in it, the angle of the joint affects the torque developed in the joint. This latter effect is a straightforward result of the fact that different directions of pull result in varying mechanical advantage. The point is illustrated in Figure 4.1 which depicts a schematized version of the elbow joint. It can be seen that since a given amount of pull by the biceps muscle has the greatest effect when it acts at right angles to the forearm, a stronger lift can be produced when the elbow is bent than when the arm is straight (see E4).

For the movement control system to act efficiently these factors which intervene to modify the consequences of a given efferent signal from brain to muscle have to be taken into account and appropriate compensatory alterations made to the efferent signal. The critical information which is necessary for these compensations concerns the tension already being developed in the muscle and the angle at which the joint is set. It is clear that proprioception, through a combination of the tendon and joint receptor systems, can provide this information.

This discussion of factors which can intervene between the signal leaving the brain and the effect produced on the environment highlights the essential problem of preserving a relation between intent and effect. There are processes identified in perception which preserve the identity of certain properties which may be subjected to transformation. For example size estimates are preserved even though the distance of the object and hence the size of the image of that object on the retina may vary. Similar preserving mechanisms operate for shape and slope, and for object colour and illumination. They are called constancy mechanisms and serve a vital function in stabilizing our internal model of the external world. By analogy with these perceptual constancy mechanisms which act to preserve the relation between object and percept, Legge and Pottinger (1968) postulated and sought to examine the properties of a *motor* constancy mechanism with the analogous function of maintaining a relation between intention and action.

The study was a limited one and only examined the elbow joint. It was found that subjects were unable to take joint angle and muscle length into account when instructed to match angular torque (as measured by fixing their arms in a piece of apparatus which prevented the elbow angle changing except under experimental control). This seemed to indicate that subjects were unable to compensate for the state of the joint by modulating the amplitude of their efferent signals, and therefore provided no evidence at all for the existence of a motor constancy system.

However, a second experiment led to a different conclusion. In this subjects were required to bend their elbow joints to different degrees and the experiment was arranged to discover how their performance was affected by the starting angle of the joint. This task is much closer to the everyday movements that are used to manipulate the environment and it was found that very good compensation for joint angle was effected. The authors concluded that a motor constancy mechanism does exist but that it operates by temporal (or frequency) modulation rather than amplitude modulation. In other words the mechanical efficiency of the muscle-joint system is compensated for by altering the length of time for which particular forces are developed in the muscles, not by modulating the levels of muscle tension.

Summary

What impact does all this have for our model? First, it establishes that the sensory modalities which transmit information about the target and object may be a distance sense like vision, but in certain circumstances may be proprioception. In fact, proprioception will be the preferred modality for object information in ball games simply because vision will be engaged by the rapidly moving target. Secondly, proprioception will be absolutely essential in the assembly of the implicit response and in the operation of the stage that produces the efferent signals that activate the muscles. Thus there are essential feedback loops carrying information from the effector muscles and joints back to the mechanisms that control them. Thirdly, we have identified the need for a mechanism, tentatively called a motor constancy mechanism, which will ensure that variations in the state of the effector system will be adequately compensated in the specification of the implicit response. The function of this motor constancy mechanism is to compensate for variations in the physical state of the effectors and thereby to seek to preserve a close relation between action and intent.

5
On speed and accuracy

It is common sense that in most situations going too fast is a prescription for making errors. Likewise an obsessional concern to avoid errors means going slower. Hence the saying 'more haste less speed'. Frequently the advice given to learners is to get it right and to speed up performance only after sufficient accuracy has been attained. This is obviously essential advice to people learning to drive, for example, since uncontrolled speed may quickly result in injury or death (see E4). There are circumstances, however, where performance is assessed as a function of both spatial accuracy and temporal accuracy, and speed of response may then be as important as accuracy. The tennis serve is one such example. It is necessary to produce co-ordinated movements of both arms so that the tennis racquet moves in an arc which intersects the path of the ball that has been thrown up with the other hand. The speed with which the ball falls is determined by gravity so a successful serve can only be achieved by adjusting the racquet movement to correspond to the flight of the ball. It is not possible simply to slow down all the components of this skill because if one did so the ball would fall to the ground before it was hit. In other words success here depends upon a particular combination of speed and accuracy.

Investigations of perceptual-motor skills have done little, as yet, to reveal the underlying processes which are responsible for the temporal coordination of the elements of skilled movements. So far most research effort has been directed instead at the problem of accuracy rather than timing. As a result, time features in these considerations in terms of how long it takes to achieve a given degree of accuracy. We shall not explore its more complex role in the coordination of components of movements with each other and with the external demands of the task. Within this more limited area a considerable amount of knowledge has now been amassed about the trade-off between speed and accuracy in making simple movements to stationary targets.

Fitts' Law

The first attempt to offer a coherent account of how long it takes to make a movement of specified amplitude (distance) and accuracy (tolerance of error) was made by Fitts (1954). He proposed an exact statement of how the time to execute an aiming movement is increased by the distance it has to go, movement amplitude, and the accuracy that is necessary to hit the target. He specified this in the following equation:

$$\text{movement time, MT} = a + b \log_2 \left(\frac{2A}{W} \right)$$

where A is movement amplitude and W is the width of the target (in the direction of the movement) and a and b are coefficients.

Leaving aside the reasons which led to the choice of this particular relation, it is encouraging to record that the relation describes data very well. Fitts conducted a number of experiments using various tasks. These included 'dotting' repeatedly from side to side between two targets, and transferring rings from vertical pegs on one side of a horizontal board to pegs on the other. The tasks all involved reciprocating movements across the front of the body. Task difficulty was altered by changing the distance between targets and by altering the target size or, in the ring and peg tasks, the tolerance of error for correct positioning. As a further variation the stylus used in the 'dotting' task was varied in weight from a few ounces to two pounds. Other researchers have extended the range of tasks to include setting rotary knobs to particular readings. In all these tasks the basic equation Fitts proposed gives a highly satisfactory account of the speed – amplitude – accuracy relation. It is not surprising, therefore, that it has been called Fitts' Law.

One feature of Fitts' original tasks that might be criticized was that the movements involved were repetitive and no record was made of the movement time and accuracy of individual movements. Only the total time to complete a given number of responses was measured and this time could be complexly determined. For instance, total time might include planning (reaction) time as well as execution (movement) time and so the overall relation might be contaminated by the effects on planning time of the accuracy that was required. This difficulty was

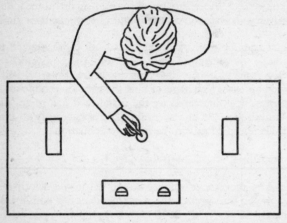

Fig. 5.1 *Bird's eye view of subject in Fitts' and Peterson's (1964) experiment. One of the two lights in front of him will be lit and thus indicate whether he is to aim at the left- or right-hand target. He is holding a stylus in contact with a circular 'home' plate. Time spent preparing to move after the light is lit (reaction time) and time spent 'in the air' (movement time) are separately measured.*

avoided by Fitts and Peterson (1964) who reported several experiments in which individual aiming movements were recorded. Reaction times and movement times were separately measured. Their apparatus is sketched in Figure 5.1. It will be seen that the targets were rectangular metal plates so that the 'accuracy' under investigation was the accuracy *in the same direction as the movement was made* (that is, the length of the movement) not the accuracy of aim. The same was true in Fitts' original 'dotting' task. Clearly the pin and ring transfer tasks involved both 'aim' and 'length' but it turns out that the principal limiting factor in these tasks is length accuracy – aim accuracy generally appears to be somewhat greater anyway. The task presented to the subject was, on a particular trial, to respond to either the left- or the right-hand target depending upon which of two lights came on. Subjects knew the distances and sizes of the targets in advance, but they did not know which of two targets they would have to hit.

The results of this experiment are summarized in Figure 5.2. It can be seen that task difficulty (based on the ratio of the distance moved to the accuracy of movement required) had a systematic and very considerable effect on *movement* time (a

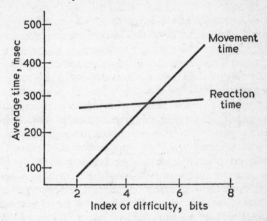

Fig. 5.2 *Movement time and reaction time as a function of difficulty of the response movement. Index of difficulty $= \log_2(2A/W)$, where A is distance to target and W is width of target* (after Fitts and Peterson, 1964).

steep slope) whereas the effect of task difficulty on *reaction* (planning) time, though systematic, is negligible. Therefore this experiment implies that the relations obtained using repetitive movements may be interpreted as relations involving movement time rather than planning time. There is no doubt that Fitts' equation provides an excellent description of data. It is a lot less clear how this relation is to be interpreted.

One possibility is to treat the function simply as a description of the overall performance of the underlying response-control processes and not to expect the functional equation above to reveal just what those processes are. To this more limited

63

end the equation can be used to provide a measure of performance in the same way as the Hick-Hyman choice reaction time function was used to deduce the information processing rate of the choice mechanism in Chapter 2. In the case of Fitts' Law the slope of the movement time function in Figure 5.2 implies an information processing rate of about 14 bits per second, and this value could be used as a measure of the movement-control performance that the subject achieved.

One important virtue of Fitts' equation is that it incorporates both speed and accuracy. In so doing it provides a convenient measure that reflects total performance in a single number.

Successive corrections models

A plausible interpretation of the Fitts' Law function is based upon the idea that the aiming movement is kept under 'continuous' control and corrections are instigated during its execution. This view is based upon observations of the actual course of aiming movements and the discovery that, in general, movements comprise an initial period of rapid acceleration followed by a longer period of varying degrees of deceleration. It follows that the first part of the journey towards the target is completed rapidly and the target is then approached ever more slowly. One observed pattern is that approximately equal periods of time are spent on successively halving the remaining distance to the target. A successive correction model of the processes underlying Fitts' Law was originally advanced by Crossman and Goodeve (1963) in an unpublished paper. Keele (1968) has taken up their basic idea and developed it systematically. He shows how Fitts' equation may be derived from the performance of a system which monitors the execution of movements and implements corrections to ensure their accuracy to whatever degree is necessary.

The argument makes two basic assumptions. These are that each correction takes the same amount of time and that the improvement in accuracy following a correction is likewise a constant. The latter assumption needs some explication. The idea is that the motor programme determining a movement cannot do so with perfect accuracy. The accuracy that can be achieved is a proportion of the distance to be moved. So, for example, if the accuracy achievable is 10 per cent, a 10 cm movement will land within 10 per cent (that is 1 cm) of the target. A further correction would enable this 'error' of 1 cm to be reduced to 10 per cent of 1 cm which is 0·1 cm, and so on.

In Keele's development the correction mechanism is considered to operate repeatedly until the accuracy defined by the last correction is within the tolerance permitted by the task, essentially the width of the target. He shows mathematically how the number of corrections necessary to ensure hitting a target is determined by its distance (A) and size (W). With the addition of a further assumption that each correction takes the same amount of time, he derives an equation which is identical to that proposed by Fitts.

Keele goes on to show that if the time to make a correction is assumed to be 260 ms (after Keele and Posner, 1968) and the proportional accuracy of an uncorrected response is 7 per cent (after Vince, 1948) his model would 'predict' the value of the slope of the Fitts' Law function observed by Fitts and Peterson. This would appear to provide convincing support for the successive corrections model of Fitts' Law.

However, Keele's development of the model is incomplete. The only specification of movement time is the number of corrections applied to the movement. Since this can only be a whole number, it follows that though the equation appears to permit movement time to vary continuously, in fact it can only take values that are multiples of the time to make a simple correction. In other words the successive corrections model predicts that movement times can only take a few particular values and that they increase in a stepwise fashion rather than continuously.

This difficulty can be surmounted by developing a model which specifies in much greater detail the physical characteristics of initial responses and subsequent corrections. It then becomes plain that even without any corrections at all execution time will be a function of both distance covered and accuracy achieved and that this relation is a continuous one. Combining this feature with the successive corrections model then offers a satisfactory account of Fitts' Law in terms of plausible underlying mechanisms. One of the fundamental assumptions is that movements are corrected once every quarter of a second and with this interval between corrections there is the strong implication that the basis for corrections is visual feedback about the ongoing movement. A subordinate assumption, and one that seems self-evident on analysis, is that all modulations of the effector mechanisms are essentially predictive. That is they are calculated to bring about some specific end result at a predicted time *in the future*. Skilled responses are the result of executing motor programmes devised to meet future situations, not just simple reactions to present and immediately past events. This predictive principle in movement control is one of the most remarkable features of the system and a defining characteristic of skill.

Non-visual control of movements

Fine-grain analysis of aiming movements reveals a superimposed rapid oscillation or tremor. This consists of small irregular movements occurring about ten times per second (that is a frequency of 10 Hz). It is interesting to speculate about its origin. Given the results of experiments by Keele and Posner (1968) and Beggs and Howarth (1970) it is now clear that corrections based on visual information cannot be implemented until about 250 ms after that information is available. Thus visually based corrections are unlikely to provide an explanation of tremor.

There are three other possible sources of high frequency irregularities. These are centrally computed modulations based on proprioceptive feedback, centrally computed modulations based on outflow monitoring, and peripheral modulations originating at the level of the effectors and not involving the central computing mechanism at all.

Very much less is known about how long it takes to process proprioceptive feedback than visual feedback. However, estimates of reaction time to proprioceptive signals suggest that though they are shorter than reaction times to visual signals, the saving is probably not more than about 50–70 ms. Thus the frequency with which corrections could be instituted on the basis of proprioceptive signals about the accuracy of the ongoing response is unlikely to be much greater than the corresponding frequency for visual feedback. The balance of probabilities makes proprioceptively based centrally computed modulations an unlikely explanation of tremor.

Outflow monitoring
The second possibility is somewhat more likely. It is based on the idea that the central computing system can monitor its

outflow and use this information for early detection of errors, even before they have become evident in overt responses. The plausibility of this general idea rests on the fact that correction responses in choice reaction are frequently much faster than initial choices, and introspective reports that one sometimes 'knows' one is going to make a mistake even before the response has been emitted. Rabbitt (1966) has described a number of the characteristics of error responses, error detection and error-correcting responses. The most striking aspect of his data was that error-correcting responses had typically shorter latencies than normal responses, and sometimes very much shorter. There were even instances of the correcting responses being initiated before the error had been displayed to the subject. Unless one is to accept that these fast corrections were based on proprioceptive feedback, an explanation that has already been dismissed as unlikely, centrally based error-detection has to be postulated.

In terms of our model (see p. 18) there are two main central outputs that could be monitored and used as a basis for error-detection. These are the required object modulation (ROM) and the implicit response (IR). One would expect that detection of an inappropriate ROM would lead to earlier error correction than detection of a wrong IR, but both would lead to faster corrections than errors detected on the basis of visual or proprioceptive feedback. However, it is questionable whether tremor could be accounted for in these terms. Although error correction based on outflow monitoring would eliminate some of the processing time otherwise involved, it would require access to the same processes which are used in visually based movement control. The resulting competition would cause interference between these two activities unless both motor outflow feedback and visual or proprioceptive feedback could somehow be combined. On balance, though this source of 10 Hz modulation is not completely ruled out, it does not commend itself unreservedly.

Peripheral servo-mechanisms

The third alternative is the most likely, mainly because it is limited to the effector system and makes no processing demands on the earlier computing mechanisms. It rests on the conception of a servo-mechanism similar to that which is involved in power-steering and power-braking systems in vehicles. A mechanism of this kind is believed to control the activity of muscles and to help ensure that they do as they are told. The reason for fitting power-braking and power-steering to vehicles is so that a relatively weak control signal from the driver is sufficient to control the vehicle. With these aids the power that has to be exerted on the brake pedal and steering wheel can be dramatically reduced so that, in principle, a job that otherwise would require the strength of a gorilla can be accomplished by a fragile nymph. The basic principle is that the driver 'tells' the 'slave' part of the servo system to adopt a particular state, such as a given amount of turn of the road-wheels, and the slave system then uses another source of power to cause the road-wheels to change direction. The signal that goes to the slave system is called a reference signal or demand signal since it

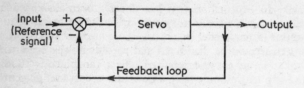

Fig. 5.3 *Diagram of negative feedback controlled servo. The output is fed back and compared with the input (reference signal). The difference between these (i) is fed to the servo which then responds until i becomes zero. In this circuit the output will become matched to the input.*

specifies a required state. The slave system is then constructed in such a way as to change itself until this required state is achieved. The slave system alters automatically whenever its state differs from the state defined by the reference signal. However, it stops changing when it matches the reference signal. The operating principle which brings about this particular function is called negative feedback. Its operation is illustrated in Figure 5.3.

The input signal to the servo is the reference signal. The reference signal might be the angle of turn of the steering wheel of a bus, the output from the system might be the direction of the road-wheels. Both these signals are angles. The servo has access to a source of power which enables the work to be done which is necessary to alter the direction of the road-wheels. Control of this external power is obtained by comparing the angle fed back from the output of the system and comparing it with the reference angle which was input to the system. In fact the output signal is subtracted from the input reference signal and the *difference* is fed to the servo which works on this difference and acts so as to reduce it to zero. It is so constructed, therefore, that whenever output and reference match, the system is inactive, but whenever there is a difference between them the system strives to remove it. This mode of operation produces two consequences. First, it means that except when the system is active the output will match the reference signal, and any change in reference signal will be reflected eventually in the output. Secondly, it means that should any external disturbance tend to alter the output of the system (such as a pot-hole which may tend to knock the car's wheels out of line) the system will automatically act to restore its original value. In this sense the feedback controlled system is stabilized against outside influences which threaten to distort its performance.

This basic concept, negative feedback, lies at the heart of a modern discipline, *cybernetics*, which is concerned with the engineering of control systems. Its name stems from a Greek word, cybernetos, which is usually translated as 'steersman'. This rather nicely pinpoints the guidance principle of control. However, there is another feature of these systems which is not so obvious. They are self-correcting and act as if they are goal-directed. Their 'goal' is the reference signal which they strive to match.

The apparent goal-direction of negative feedback controlled systems derives from their inevitable tendency to change to match a demand signal. Such behaviour does not, of course, require that purpose be inferred and certainly not consciousness. This becomes self-evident when one remembers that the thermostat which controls the domestic oven or central heating system is actually a negative feedback control device. The reference or demand signal for these systems is set manually (the regulo number or temperature setting). The thermostat then operates to increase heat production until the temperature specified by it is attained. The heater is then shut down but when the temperature drops again (as it inevitably will) the thermostat responds to the difference between required and actual temperature and switches on the heater once more. Most domestic irons also incorporate this kind of system. Some of them have a little light that glows when the heater is operating and then goes out when it shuts down. This example is a particularly good one for our purposes because one can actually *see* another property of feedback controlled systems – they hunt (see E4).

Hunting is the continuous variation in the output produced by the system. One moment it may be greater than required, the next moment less, even when a constant demand signal is applied to it. Though negative feedback tends to stabilize the system and protect it from the effects of unwanted interference, it does not make the system static. This is quite obvious when looking at the pilot light of one's domestic iron. Even when the reference or demand signal is constant, the output instead of taking a fixed value oscillates about the desired value. The period of this oscillation and the size of the fluctuations depends upon the detailed construction of the system but it is impossible to produce one with a perfectly stable output. In fact, it turns out to be undesirable to eliminate these fluctuations entirely. Systems with only small, very low frequency oscillations are comparatively slow in responding to changes in the reference signal. It follows that if an efficient response to variation in demand is to be attained a relatively high frequency of oscillation in output must also be a characteristic of the system.

There is an obvious similarity between the continuous motion which is tremor and the continuous oscillation which is an intrinsic feature of these negative-feedback-controlled mechanisms. This similarity is the basis of the hypothesis that tremor is due to the operation of such a system. The next step is to discover any other evidence that would make this hypothesis more than just plausible. Physiological data are available that does just that.

Muscle-spindle servo. We have already described the joint receptor system, which signals to the brain the angles of the joints in the body, and the tendon receptor system that responds to the tension developed in the muscles. These have been identified as the sources of proprioceptive information which apparently serve an essential role in the initial planning and subsequent correction of movements. In addition to these two receptor systems there is another system, the muscle-spindle system, which is sometimes included as part of proprioception

70

but which is probably better regarded as a system in its own right.

The muscle spindles are small but very complex structures which lie in parallel with muscle fibres. Each spindle comprises two functionally different parts. One is a micro-muscle, the other is a stretch receptor in some ways similar to the tendon receptors. The layout of these two parts of the spindle is such that if the ends of the spindle are prevented from moving, contraction of the micro-muscle increases the tension on the stretch-sensitive element causing it to emit signals. Relaxation of the micro-muscle decreases the tension and the frequency of signals from the stretch-sensitive element diminishes. This dual-character of the muscle spindle, motor and sensory, is matched by its dual innervation. There are afferent nerves leading from the stretch receptor portion of the spindle and small diameter, so-called gamma efferent nerves leading to the micro-muscle.

The key to the function of muscle spindles lies in their relation to muscle fibres. They are so placed that when their associated muscle fibres contract the tension across the spindle decreases and when the fibre relaxes the tension increases (see Fig. 5.4). This happens because the groups of muscles which control the angles of joints are arranged in opposition. This is seen most clearly for simple hinge-like joints such as the elbow. There are several muscle groups pulling both ways but the major bending forces are from the contraction of the biceps and the major straightening forces come from the triceps muscle groups. The organization of muscle activity is so arranged that contraction of one group normally coincides with a corresponding degree of relaxation of the antagonist muscles.

It follows from this reciprocal action that when a muscle relaxes it lengthens under the tension developed in the simultaneously contracting antagonist muscles. When this happens the associated muscle spindles will be subjected to increased tension that will be signalled by the stretch-sensitive receptors that they contain. Alternatively, when a muscle contracts it shortens thereby reducing the tension across the associated muscle-spindles. However, the micro-muscle in the spindle can also cause the activity of its stretch-sensitive receptor to change. So the output from these receptors is a complex function of the activity of the micro-muscles in the spindles and of the surrounding muscle fibres. Muscle spindles are therefore rather

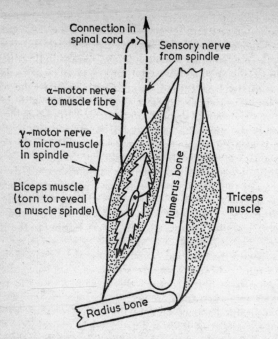

Fig. 5.4 *Diagram of an elbow joint and the biceps and triceps muscles which control its angle. The biceps has been 'torn' open to reveal a schematic muscle-spindle. The spindle comprises a micro-muscle activated by gamma-motor nerves and a stretch-sensitive element which responds to stretch produced either directly by contraction of the micro-muscle or indirectly by the antagonist muscle (triceps in this example). Activity in the spindle sensory nerve is transferred in the spinal cord to the main alpha-motor nerve to the muscle fibre. The resulting contraction of the muscle fibre relieves the tension across the spindle.*

poorly placed to serve as proprioceptors in the sense we previously described. The information issuing from them cannot be easily interpreted unambiguously. However, it makes them ideal as the essential elements in a negative feedback control system.

The arrangement of muscle fibre and muscle spindle which is the basis of this servo-mechanism is shown in Figure 5.4. The critical additional feature shown in this diagram is the connection of the output from the muscle spindle to the main efferent nerve to the muscle fibre. This has the effect that increasing activity in the spindle stretch receptor causes increased contraction of the muscle fibre and vice versa. The best known example of the operation of this feedback loop is the patellar tendon reflex. A tap on the tendon just below the knee causes a brief but massive increase in the tension across muscle spindles in the quadriceps muscle in the front of the thigh, resulting in a large but short-lived discharge to the thigh muscle itself and the characteristic kick ensues.

It is clear that there are now two possible routes by which signals can bring about contractions of the muscle fibre. They can travel by the direct route descending the alpha, large diameter fibres or by an indirect route. The latter route involves the gamma efferent fibres producing contraction of the micromuscle in the spindle which causes increased activity in the spindle stretch receptor that is conveyed via the feedback loop to the main alpha nerves controlling the muscle fibres. Clearly these two routes are not equivalent. Even if other factors did not intervene the indirect route looks like taking somewhat longer than the direct route. Moreover, the relative slowness of the indirect, feedback route is aggravated by the fact that nerve impulses travel slower in small diameter, gamma fibres than they do in large diameter, alpha fibres. Anatomical investigation reveals that the alpha fibres extend up to the brain so that the existence of the indirect route is not absolutely necessary. The direct route would appear to be quicker and therefore more efficient.

However, the existence of the indirect feedback route provides a very important property that the direct route lacks. The gamma efferent signal can act as a reference signal which will determine the activity of the main muscle fibre. If it tends to contract too much the feedback from the spindle will reduce its contraction and if not enough increase it. In other words the muscle-spindle feedback loop will act to stabilize the activity of the muscle fibre, causing it to settle on a value determined by the gamma efferent signal to the muscle. The advantage of a peripheral stabilization system of this kind is obvious. Gibbs (1970) takes the example of a man walking over uneven ground. The variation in level will be a disturbing influence to the coordinated muscle contractions which walking involves. However, the muscle-spindle feedback control system enables compensatory changes to be implemented peripherally without the intervention of central correction computing mechanisms. This delegation of control function has obvious advantages in terms of the efficiency of the total system.

As we have said earlier a universal characteristic of servo-mechanisms is that they hunt. Their output oscillates continuously and this is the price that is paid for the rapidity with which they react to new demands. There seems no reason to suppose that the muscle-spindle negative feedback servo should be any different and oscillating output is therefore to be expected. It would appear to be quite clearly manifested as tremor. In short, an adequate explanation of tremor would seem to lie in the nature of the peripheral servo-mechanism which is the final processing system before movements become observable.

Accuracy of aiming

At the beginning of this chapter the relation between speed and accuracy was discussed and Fitts' Law was analysed in some depth. The point was made then that the tasks which lend support to Fitts' Law are ones in which the subject's ability to control the extent or length of his movement is the principal limitation on his speed of performance. However, the accuracy of aim is another aspect of movement control and is not adequately investigated in the kinds of experiments that have been conducted in the Fitts' Law tradition.

Two-dimensional aiming

This distinction between the aim and extent of movements is made more obvious by considering a way of investigating both. Such an experiment was reported by Begbie (1959). Subjects were instructed to make aiming movements with pencils on sheets of paper from a home starting-point to a target point marked on the sheet. This technique, by restricting subjects' movements to two dimensions instead of the three involved in the Fitts' tasks and by using pencils, meant that each aiming movement left a permanent record of its track. Begbie then considered errors of aim and errors of extent separately. Errors of aim reflected the angular error of the direction of the movement. Errors of extent were basically overshoot and under-shoot errors.

Errors of extent are probably mainly caused by an inappropriate choice of muscle contractions that either terminates a movement too soon or prolongs it unnecessarily. Errors of aim, however, are the result of the particular set of muscles chosen to be contracted and the balance of activity distributed amongst them. Fitts' Law may be described as the consequence of initial and corrected choices of accelerations and decelerations in a given direction; errors of aim cannot be considered in the same way.

In an important paper Drury (1971) brought together some data about aiming accuracy and its relation to movement time and the distance moved. He also constructed a mathematically expressed model based upon essentially the same ideas of a successive correction process which Keele (1968) applied to errors of extent.

It turns out that whereas Fitts found that a logarithmic function was appropriate to relate movement time to errors of extent, where errors of aim are concerned linear relations are more commonly found. For example, if the time spent moving is virtually constant and no visually based corrections are made, the further one moves the bigger the error. This would appear to support the view that aim error can be considered as an angular deviation from the perfect aim line, so that the further the movement proceeds from its starting point the greater the distance between the line tracked by the movement and the ideal line.

A less obvious relation is found between movement time and aim error when movements are of a fixed length. In this case there is a simple inverse relation between time and accuracy. Generally, the faster the movement the greater the error, and this relation is also linear.

Three-dimensional aiming

A slightly different approach to the problem of aiming accuracy has been adopted by Howarth and Beggs and their colleagues. Their principal task is an analogue of throwing darts. Subjects are instructed to make aiming movements with a pencil at a vertical target up to eighteen inches in front of them. We have already mentioned that Beggs and Howarth used this task to estimate the last moment during the course of a movement that a visually based correction could be initiated. The task has also been used by Howarth, Beggs and Bowden (1971) to examine the relation between accuracy and distance, concentrating on the last quarter of a second of movement leading up to impact on the target.

Howarth *et al.* paced their subjects so that the actual approach to the target was at various speeds and the last quarter of a second of movement represented varying distances. They also measured accuracy in two dimensions as scatter on the target, rather than in one dimension as most previous workers had done. This difference in task and measurement, and the fact that Howarth's subjects were making movements paced by the experimenter rather than at their own pace, makes a direct comparison between Drury's and Howarth's models difficult, but in general terms it appears that the relations identified by Drury are confirmed by Howarth.

There is, however, one important feature in Howarth's equations which Drury omits. This is a term which represents the inaccuracy of landing on the target which is attributable to tremor. Consider a subject with a very considerable tremor. He might have an average aim that was perfect but superimposed upon this would be the wobble in the air from his hand tremor. He might be lucky and land on the bull's eye but he is more than likely to miss it.

Howarth and his colleagues have reported a number of experiments which have allowed numerical estimates to be made of the wobble attributable to tremor and of the angular accuracy of aim. In their experiments in which subjects had to strike a vertical target more or less at arm's length the tremor refers to the unsupported extended arm and so is likely to be larger than under other conditions. A tremor amplitude of about 2 mm is required by their model and this is a credible figure. It is also interesting to note that for this task they find consistently an angular accuracy of aim of about a third of a degree. This latter figure presumably reflects the essential accuracy with which aiming movements can be executed and is composed of inaccuracies of both perception and response generation. Considering the complexity of the processes that intervene this degree of accuracy seems remarkable.

Summary

This chapter has examined the relation between speed and accuracy of graded responses made to stationary targets. It transpires that movements may be inaccurate either in extent or in aim, and these two forms of inaccuracy are governed by different laws. Errors of extent are attributed to inaccuracies in controlling the stopping of movements, while errors of aim can be accounted for in terms of the initial angular error of aim and the distance moved before correction. Both aspects of movement are controlled by mechanisms that probably implement corrections to ongoing movements every quarter of a second. These corrections appear to be based mainly upon visual feedback.

Irregularities in the course of movements are also observed to occur more frequently at about ten per second. This tremor is attributed to the natural oscillation of a negative feedback servo-mechanism. This servo is based on muscle spindles and provides the final peripheral motor-control mechanism that helps to stabilize motor performance.

6
Matching on the move

In the previous chapter we considered how movements are made to a stationary target. We saw how if they were accomplished very quickly then the accuracy achieved was attributable almost entirely to the accuracy with which the response programme had been assembled prior to the response being executed. In this case accuracy is strictly limited by speed of response and the distance moved. Real-life versions of tasks like that would include playing darts, bowling and shove ha'penny.

Slower responses may last long enough for corrections to be superimposed on the original specification of the movement. This will be mandatory if the required degree of accuracy is very high and cannot be attained with an unmodified response programme. It is possible in some aiming situations that although a sufficiently slow but unmodified response could attain the required degree of accuracy, it would be more efficient to make a fast initial response and then correct it. In any case correction of the initial programme appears to occur repeatedly for as long as the movement lasts and at intervals of about a quarter of a second.

It is a logical step to move from the situation in which a stationary target is attained by a mutiply corrected response to that where the target is in motion and responses have to be produced to match that motion.

Laboratory tracking tasks divide conveniently into pursuit and compensatory versions (see p. 15). In *pursuit* tracking a target is displayed as is an object which has to be superimposed or aligned with it. The subject controls the object more or less directly but has no control over the target. This means that he can appreciate directly what the problem is that he has to solve. In *compensatory* tracking the experimenter-controlled perturbations and the subject's own responses are combined to influence a single index which he is instructed to maintain at a constant value. One way of conceiving of the relation between these two tasks is to think of compensatory tracking as displaying the *relation* between target and object instead of the absolute states of each as in pursuit tracking. Real-life situations in which a displayed value has to be maintained while being subject to unpredictable disturbances exemplify compensatory tracking. Many industrial control tasks fall into this category.

The principal advantage of laboratory tracking tasks is that the problem presented to the subject can be deliberately chosen and closely controlled. For example, by presenting various kinds of motion of the target, the subject's limitations in responding can be determined and insight into the processes underlying performance may be gained. They also have the great advantage, for the same reason, that tasks can be devised that are simple enough to be understood by the experimenter. Many real-life situations are so complex, and involve so many different kinds of difficulty for subjects, that analysing them is virtually impossible.

Pacing and timing

It should be said, however, that laboratory analogues of real-life tracking-type situations usually differ from them in one perhaps vital respect. Most real-life situations allow the operator to choose his own pace of working. This is certainly true of driving and, of course, this option is exercised so that road speed is reduced when negotiating a hazard of some kind. Few laboratory tasks offer this facility. There is some advantage in not doing so. By imposing a speed of working on the subject the difficulty of the task presented to him can be controlled and his limitations more clearly exposed. It is generally only by discovering the upper limits of performance that results can be obtained which reveal aspects of the processes underlying that performance. However, a paced task of this kind is not different from all real-life situations. Navigating a ship is theoretically a self-paced task, but the time lag involved in changing speed is so great that for all practical purposes it is paced. It takes a super-tanker several miles to come to a halt from a cruising speed of 15 to 20 knots. As Poulton (1974) remarks, the most difficult part of flying is to land the plane. It is this manœuvre which is the most severely restricting. The pilot has to approach along a narrowly defined flight-path at a precisely defined speed. Deviation in any way may spell disaster.

There are a number of other situations which fall between aiming at a stationary target and tracking a moving one. These involve the acquisition of a moving target. They include many aspects of ball games, even catching a ball. The critical feature is that they are paced situations which are time limited. There is one particular moment in time when target and object must coincide. The pacing is perhaps most onerous in these tasks because the timing of the final acquisition movement is absolutely critical.

Tracking as matching

In real-life tracking situations the movement of the target is usually more or less unpredictable. The less predictable it is the more difficult the task. If the target moves in a perfectly predictable way the problem is a close relation of the movement towards a stationary target, with some added complications. These are essentially that instead of first having to match position, it is also necessary to match velocity, and perhaps acceleration and even rate of change of acceleration as well. If any one of these aspects of the target's movement is not matched, the overall match that is required will not be achieved. For example, in order to cycle beside a friend both relative spatial position (side by side) and velocity are critical. Riding at the same speed but ten feet behind is no good. Neither is riding at his side but at a faster speed, because shortly afterwards you will be riding in front of him and as time goes by you will get further and further apart. Some tracking tasks are devised in order to examine this kind of performance.

The difficulty of the task is considerably increased by making the motion of the target unpredictable. It is then necessary to match every movement of the target and, if perfect accuracy is to be achieved, every response has to be perfectly calculated.

The effect of introducing unpredictable variations in the target's motion is very similar to that of imposing a strict time at which a stationary target has to be acquired. Both situations have the characteristic that if accuracy is not achieved in a very short space of time it will never be achieved. Of course, the continuous tracking version allows the subject to make another attempt but this will be aimed at the target in a new position and is functionally equivalent to a new and different acquisition task.

Measuring the accuracy of performance

These considerations lead inevitably to the problem of the criteria of accuracy which govern performance. In ball-catching or tennis 'a miss is as good as a mile'. There is no advantage in a near miss. In tracking the demands are different. Ideally one should be 'on-target' *all the time* and so if the responses necessary to get on target at one moment militate against being on target for some time afterwards, it might be just as well to forego that brief period of perfect accuracy. Clearly there is room here for strategy. Unlike real-life situations laboratory tasks are devised so that perfect performance cannot be maintained indefinitely. The best is some kind of imperfection. A particular score might be achieved in several ways. For example, a period exactly on target coupled with a period way off target might receive the same score as a single period never exactly on target but never far away from it. Real-life situations tend to favour the latter. In driving it is far better to wander a little from the best road position than to maintain it some of the time but mow down pedestrians on the pavement now and again. Astute choice of scoring method is needed if a laboratory task is to encourage the same conservative strategy which characterizes driving. An obvious solution to this problem is to penalize large errors disproportionately. Pedestrian deaths have this effect on the driver. This is achieved in the laboratory by using the scoring system preferred by Poulton (1974) after having analysed the advantages and disadvantages of the plethora of indices that have been used during the last thirty years.

Root mean square error (RMS). The method Poulton recommends is to calculate the root mean square error (RMS). This is calculated by measuring errors as frequently as necessary (or possible), squaring the measures, adding these squares together, then dividing them by the number of errors entered into the calculation and finally finding the square root of that average. RMS has several advantages over other competing indices but one of the more important is that by using the *square* of the recorded mismatch big errors have disproportionately more effect on the final score than small errors.

The principal alternative measure of performance, at least in terms of popularity amongst researchers, is 'time-on-target'. This is a simple measure to obtain in most circumstances which is technically easier to calculate than RMS. Unfortunately it has several severe drawbacks. All errors are treated identically. The index takes no account of how far off-target a response is. In addition the size of the target is critical: big targets lead to higher scores than small targets. Time-on-target is obviously better than no measure at all but fails to reflect important features of performance that are incorporated appropriately in the RMS index. Perhaps now is the time to point out that some of the advantages of a particular index depend on what the subject thinks is being used to assess his performance. If he understands that large discrepancies will be penalized very heavily and that small ones are not much worse than being smack on target, then he can choose a strategy which is appropriate. If, on the other hand, he applies a time-on-target strategy and an RMS index is used to assess his performance he will clearly not appear to be performing as efficiently. In real life people can evaluate what is important in a situation and frame their strategies accordingly. Laboratory tasks often lack intrinsic indications of the relative importance of different aspects of importance. So they have to be provided unless the experimental subject is to be left uncertain as to what he should do. Unless his uncertainty is removed the data that the experiment generates will be made messy because different subjects may interpret the task in different ways.

Tracking targets moving in particular ways

Laboratory tracking tasks are usually used to investigate a particular hypothesis about performance. It may be concerned with the form of the display, the nature of the controls that the subject has to manipulate, the relation between them or some more theoretical question concerning the fundamental nature of the underlying processes. The choice of the task and the details of the problem it sets the subject are critically governed by these considerations. One of the features which may be chosen in order to reveal particular aspects of the underlying processes is the course of the target. This is a specification of how the target changes in time. Most tracking tasks use visually perceived targets so the target's course describes how it changes its spatial position over time.

Predictable courses

Target courses can be grouped into two classes, regular and quasi-random. Regular courses are predictable but not necessarily simple. In contrast, quasi-random courses are unpredictable but are not completely random, for reasons that will become apparent later. The simplest regular course is one which involves sudden maintained changes of position. These are called step-tracks because the change in the target is an instantaneous step to a new position. If the target's course was written out on a long sheet of paper it would look like a series of up and down steps. A step change of the target's position demands that the subject make an acquisition movement, so performance on this task is basically the same as making corrected aiming movements. The only difference in the tracking context is that the effects of requiring different aiming responses in quick succession can be examined. Experiments like this reveal that aiming movements cannot be made more often than about four times per second. If a new response is demanded within a quarter of a second of the old, it is usually delayed. The phenomenon has been examined in detail under the heading of the psychological refractory phase (PRP), using ungraded reaction time responses more often than aiming movements (see Ch. 7).

One step more complicated than maintaining a constant spatial position is maintaining a constant velocity. This kind of course, which displays a target moving in a given direction at constant speed, is called a ramp function. Perfect tracking of this kind of course demands a match of both position and velocity. One limitation in most constant velocity courses is that the display lasts for only a limited time. A target spot on a cathode ray tube will traverse the screen in a time determined by the size of the screen and the speed of the spot but eventually it will run off the edge of the screen. The higher the velocity the sooner this will happen. Clearly the main advantage of this type of course is that one can study subjects' abilities to prepare and correct movements to match velocity.

Sine-wave courses. Perhaps the most complex of the regular courses is the sinusoidal course, or sine-wave. This course specifies a continuously changing position, velocity and acceleration of the target. In one dimension the target moves from side to side, stopping for an instant at the extremes of its excursion and moving at its highest speed midway between these extremes. Its acceleration is zero at this midpoint and maximal at the extremes – the acceleration represents a force that tends to return the target to the midpoint position. A simple everyday example, though not one restricted to one dimension, is the movement of the pendulum of a clock. The reason for including this kind of course along with the constant characteristics courses considered above is because of its regularity. Position, velocity and acceleration are continuously changing but in a perfectly regular manner, which means that, at least in theory, they are predictable. Thus, providing the tracker can produce such an output with the same amplitude and frequency of excursion, it is possible to track even this course perfectly accurately. In fact, perfect accuracy is almost impossible to attain, but subjects certainly can produce sinusoidal outputs which are corrected from time to time. They are not restricted to programming responses just in terms of constant parameters of position, velocity and acceleration. They can programme responses so that planned variations in these parameters over time are incorporated.

Quasi-random courses

In contrast to regular target courses are the infinite variety of quasi-random courses. These courses are all unpredictable to some degree and are more similar to the natural courses of real-life targets. They tax subjects' abilities to respond to varying combinations of position, velocity, acceleration and so on. In so doing, they provide information about how subjects can adjust their responses to such continuously varying situations. These courses are usually called quasi-random because they are subject to one very important constraint. Instantaneous large changes in target position are not permitted. The course is constrained so that in theory, if not in practice, the subject could track it. Step changes in position, therefore, are precluded since they demand that subjects should make control movements at an infinitely high velocity – which is, of course, not possible. A truly random selection of spatial positions is therefore prohibited.

Levels of control of movements

Analysis of tracking performance, when subjects are faced with courses of different kinds, reveals something of the nature of the motor programmes that govern their responses. Adopting a physical analysis of performance, various orders or levels of control can be defined. The lowest or zero order is positional control. At this level the motor programme would simply define a position to be achieved and the system would only be able to monitor its performance in terms of position errors. Certain patterns in performance would be expected of a system that was only a zero-order (position) control mechanism. For example, although such a system would be able to deal with courses which comprise step-wise changes of target position, anything more complex would present insuperable difficulties. In Figure 6.1 is shown the possible performance of such a hypothetical system facing a constant velocity ramp function. At each moment the system only responds to its position error. However, since every correction is towards the point where the target was in the past, and corrections can be made only inter-mittently, the track is a saw-tooth. The steeper the ramp (that is the higher the velocity of the target) the less accurate track-ing performance is.

The next level of control, first order, means being able to alter *velocity* directly and being able to match velocity. There-fore corrections can be made to the velocity of the tracking movement. A problem becomes apparent now, because a system that only matched velocity would be hopeless for a tracking task. The object might match the target in terms of velocity but this condition does not mean that the two will be superimposed. Position matching is required in addition to velocity matching if the goal of making target and object coincide is to be achieved. In Figure 6.1 is depicted the track of a system that can adjust velocity directly as well as position when faced with a target describing a constant velocity course. Obviously this system is able to perform more satisfactorily than one which is restricted to positional control.

Second-order control concerns the *acceleration* component of movement. The considerations we have spelled out for velocity control apply here too. However it is also clear that while acceleration control will confer obvious advantages in tracking a constant acceleration course, perfect tracking performance will require velocity and position matching as well. Third-order control carries the story a stage further, and perhaps one could consider higher order levels of control as well. Third order is

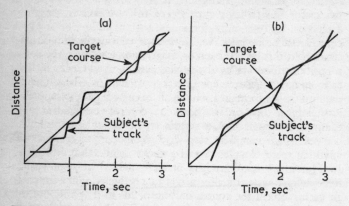

Fig. 6.1 *Representations of subjects tracking a velocity ramp function – the target moves at a constant velocity:*

(a) *the subject is 'position tracking', always correcting for just his position error;*

(b) *the subject is responding to the velocity error as well as position error.*

The step-wise pattern of corrections in (a) is a feature of situations in which the subject has no information about velocity. It may be found in records of compensatory tracking.

rate of change of acceleration and is sometimes called 'jerk'. For practical purposes it is not usual to carry an analysis of behaviour beyond third order.

The advantage of higher order levels of control is that the number of centrally computed modulations of response may be reduced. If the object is on-target an appropriate adjustment of the accelerative component of the response may be sufficient to maintain accurate tracking for several seconds. Such an adjustment could be relatively easily computed and coded. A system lacking acceleration control would need to specify a set of time-related changes in velocity to approximate the same tracking responses. They would require more complex central computations for their specification, and even then the end result would not be as satisfactory as direct control of acceleration. So higher order control imposes a lower computational load and results in smoother performance.

Orders of control in control systems

So far in this discussion we have been considering implicitly tasks in which there has been a direct relation between the control movements made by the subject and the movement of the object he has to make to coincide with the target. The simplest version of this paradigm is where the object is the hand itself, or where it is held in the hand. In the paper-strip tracking apparatus described in Chapter 1 subjects may track with a hand-held ball-point. The hand-held camera technique beloved by cinéma vérité is a slightly more complicated example of this situation. Many real-life situations, however, interpose a different relation between an operator's movements of a control and the motion of the controlled object. In other words a positional change made by the operator may cause some other kind of change to the system he is controlling. This is most commonly exemplified by consideration of vehicle control. It is nearly always the case that the basic control affected by the operator is a positional movement. It may be pressing the gas-pedal down to a particular position in a car, turning the steering wheel to a particular angle, or turning the rudder of a ship. However, the nature of these systems is different, so that positional changes of the control device have different consequences in each case.

To begin with, in none of these examples does a positional change of the control device only affect a positional change of the system. The gas-pedal in a car determines the road-speed of the car. It does so in a rather complicated way, and the final speed achieved for a given setting of the gas-pedal is dependent upon innumerable factors including the air-resistance of the car-body, the friction in the engine and transmission, and the design of the carburettor, inlet manifold and exhaust system. Nevertheless the essential thing is that the gas-pedal is a *velocity* control – not an accelerator as its common name would suggest. Perhaps even more surprising at first thought, the steering wheel of a car is a second-order (acceleration) control, and the rudder of a ship is a third-order control. Let us see how this comes about.

Consider steering a car – let's make it a Rolls-Royce, not out of snobbery or to indulge fantasy but because it has an emblem (the winged victory) on its bonnet. Imagine driving the car so that the emblem is seen against the background horizon. One can imagine now that provided the steering wheel is in its central position the emblem will be stationary with respect to some fixed point on the horizon. Now turn the steering wheel a little and hold it there, but continue to watch the emblem and its relation to that same fixed point. The emblem will move away from the reference point slowly to begin with but with ever increasing speed. In fact the emblem is accelerating away from the reference point. In order to keep the increase in distance at a constant value it is necessary to straighten up the steering wheel again. This example makes two points. First, the steering system of a car is a second-order (acceleration) control system, and secondly a second-order influence sets the level of control immediately beneath it. A given steering-wheel angle applied for a few seconds will leave a particular velocity when it is removed. If it is applied for longer it will leave a higher velocity. In order to remove the velocity introduced by the acceleration it is necessary to apply a reverse angle to the steering wheel. This is just like giving a pram a quick push (accelerating it). To stop it again it is necessary to remove the acceleration which made it start moving and match it with a deceleration to make it stop.

The order of a control system specifies the characteristics of motion which are affected by it. For example, a zero-order (positional) control system affects position directly. A first-order (velocity) control affects velocity directly, and through it, position. A second-order (acceleration) control affects acceleration directly but, in addition, velocity and position indirectly.

Steering a ship is even more complicated because ships are not as firmly connected to the sea as cars are attached to the ground. Basically ships tend to swing round about their centre point while cars tend to move in a straight line. The friction between tyres and road stops any tendency for the car to rotate. Considering this situation further we can see that whereas a car will continue in a straight line (and our Rolls-Royce emblem will move away from the reference point on the horizon at a constant velocity) the ship, even when the rudder has been returned to the amidships position, will continue to swing round and a reverse application of rudder will be necessary to stop it. This tendency to swing even after removing the rudder angle means that with respect to a fixed point on the horizon (like a lighthouse) the ship is still accelerating. We may conclude, therefore, that the rudder control of a ship is a third-order control which after it has been removed leaves the second order (acceleration) set to a new value. So this situation is just like steering a car but one order of control more complex.

Laboratory studies reveal that it is very rare that performance is improved by having first- or second-order control *instead* of zero-order control. Performance is nearly always superior when direct control of the system is possible – that is zero order. The reason is clear. If the subject has to use a first-, second- or higher order control he cannot produce a direct effect on the position of the system he is attempting to control. Though he may want to produce a positional change to the system, a positional change of his control will produce a change of the system's acceleration. Therefore he can only produce positional changes of the system indirectly. Unfortunately these features of vehicle control are natural as well as undesirable. No designer would have included them if an alternative was available.

Not surprisingly, many attempts have been made to find ways of simplifying the task of controlling systems which by their nature prohibit the use of zero-order (direct) controls. The general principles could be applied to all high-order control systems but the penalties of poor control are larger in some situations than others. Controlling aeroplanes, ships and submarines are cases in point. These are systems entailing third-order control and substantial lags in the system's response. There are two basic approaches to the problem of easing the controller's task. One is to display to him some or all of the intervening changes that ensue from his control movements (e.g. acceleration and velocity as well as position, which he is attempting to control). The other is to provide a predictor display which shows him what the system will be like several seconds ahead, assuming the current setting of the controls is maintained.

Several times in this, as well as the last chapter, we have asserted that movement control is effected intermittently rather than continuously. Though evidence for this view has now been obtained from several different sources, the original observations pointing to this conclusion were obtained by Craik (1947) and Vince (1948). The data were obtained from two different compensatory tracking tasks. One was a task in which subjects had to crank a handwheel at 1 revolution per minute in order to compensate for a steady drift of the target off-centre. The other was a more usual task in which subjects had to alter the position of a lever to compensate for various different kinds of externally introduced deflections of the target. The actual control movements which subjects made were recorded and subsequently analysed. The time between each correction of response was measured. Corrections were revealed by sudden changes in the trace of the record of control movements. These records imply two important conclusions. First, the existence of sudden alterations in responding, instead of a continuous smooth trace, reveals that corrections are implemented intermittently. Secondly, the distribution of inter-modulation times indicates that corrections are effected four times per second or less. Furthermore, Vince found that altering the rate of movement of the target, and hence the difficulty of the task, made no difference to the rate at which movements were corrected. The average reported by Vince was twice per second but this figure will have been distorted by the fact that a correction will not always make a sufficiently large change to the ongoing response to be detected. The data are congruent with the view that corrections are implemented at quarter-second intervals.

Examination of many tracking records fails to reveal intermittent corrections of this kind and it is pertinent to ask why. The answer is probably because a variety of factors may act to obscure this essential characteristic of the underlying movement control mechanism. The principal ones are inertia, the order of control and anticipation. The last two are interdependent.

The smoothing effect of inertia is fairly obvious. If the control system is heavy it is just extremely difficult to make it change its position suddenly without exerting colossal forces on it. Few tracking studies set out to use such dramatically massive controls but inertia must play some part in smoothing out the response record.

Anticipation

The smoothing effect of anticipation and the order of control exerted are less obvious factors. Poulton (1957) has described two kinds of anticipation which are relevant to this discussion. One kind, *sensory* anticipation, refers to pursuit tracking without preview (i.e. when the course cannot be seen ahead) and depends upon the subject being able to derive information from the target about its velocity and acceleration. This information can then be used to predict its future position. The other kind, *perceptual* anticipation, provides more certain knowledge over a longer time period. Perceptual anticipation is based upon either preview of the course or learning a repeating course. In either case the future position of the target is known and the subject can use this advance information in order to compute an efficient response to meet future as well as current contingencies.

These kinds of anticipation permit the effective operation of higher levels of control than would otherwise be possible. Suppose the velocity of the target is constant; then if the motor programme can match that velocity it will be a lot more efficient than if it makes a series of positional corrections, and it would lead to much smoother performance. The same advantages would arise from having sufficient information about the target's course to be able to implement a motor programme to specify an acceleration. Preview takes the situation even further into the future and may allow a programme to be prepared that defines sundry time-related modulations, smoothly executed and extending over perhaps five seconds (Poulton, 1957).

It seems inevitable that if a motor programme has been prepared which will guide the ongoing response for several seconds into the future, corrections implemented every quarter of a second are going to make only very slight alterations to the next section of the programme, though the changes further ahead in time may be more radical. One would not expect to see clear sudden alterations to the ongoing movement except very rarely. It follows that situations which permit the operation of the predictive mechanisms, and hence relatively long-term forward planning, would not show up the essential intermittency. All pursuit tracking situations permit some degree of anticipation and so will not be sensitive to intermittency. Compensatory tracking, however, provides no independent information about target motion and no preview. The opportunity for efficient prediction is reduced to a minimum. It is in these situations in which the preparation of an accurate motor programme that extends beyond the immediate present is very limited, that evidence of intermittent correction is found. On reflection it is not surprising that manifest intermittency is rare since it is evidence of inefficient functioning. It is only going to be evident when a more effective mode of operation is prevented by the nature of the task.

7
The single channel hypothesis

Science, in its quest to comprehend the apparently limitless complexity of the observations which it makes, seeks ideas that will unify them. Some might argue that it even grasps them like drowning men grasp at straws. However, it is by extending the explanatory power of unifying concepts that understanding proceeds. Thus we now have general laws describing the operation of many physical and chemical phenomena, and, increasingly, corresponding ideas in the biological sciences as well.

In the field of information processing and human performance one such unifying concept has been the notion that in many situations man acts like a single information processing channel of limited capacity. This is the single channel hypothesis. In this chapter we seek to indicate the main lines of evidence which led to and support this conceptualization of the processes underlying behaviour, and to consider some of the evidence which threatens it.

The nature of the hypothesis

Perhaps it would be as well to consider the single channel hypothesis in the context of the more obvious alternative suppositions. It will then be clearer, we hope, what the hypothesis implies and what it does not. First, let us consider the notion of 'channel'. This is rather a general purpose word to describe a route between input and output which may be just a transmission line like a telephone wire, but is much more likely to incorporate a chain of mechanisms, each responsible for a particular process. The essential character of the channel is that it can process only one set of information at a particular instant in time. If one takes the analogy of a single track railway line, only one train can exist on a particular portion of track at any given moment. Another analogy would be an automatic car-wash that can shampoo and shower only one vehicle at a time.

We are concerned with a particular kind of channel, an information processing channel, and the car-wash analogy would be closer than the railway track. Our channel is considered to transform or otherwise process the information it receives, not just convey it from one point to another (see A6). It is important also to consider the way it is limited in its capacity to process information. Twenty-five years ago single channel theory was thought of mainly as being limited in terms of its information processing rate. This limiting rate was defined technically, using the metric of information theory, and thus was measured in bits per second (see Ch. 2). However, the optimism of the 1950s may have been insufficiently cautious. Information processing may be inadequately represented by the metric of information theory, and single channel theory does not need to be constrained by its limitations.

In brief then, single channel theory asserts that in some important ways the human being when processing information does so in a limited fashion. In particular, he can process only one batch of information at a time and can do so at a limited speed.

The plausibility of this idea may become easier to assess by contemplating the more obvious alternative scheme. The simpler considerations concern the singularity of the channel and its limitations. One could conceive of a system that operated as a set of several limited channels. Such a system could process simultaneously as many different batches of information as there were channels. The capacity limitation would still restrict the throughput of information, but the system could genuinely do several things at once. If the capacity of the system were unlimited then the number of channels would be a meaningless issue since, by definition, it would deal with any processing problem instantaneously. In any case, this extreme consideration is pointless because the brain has a limited number of nerve cells and no structurally limited system is capable of unlimited function.

One issue about the information processing limitation is

worth pursuing. The simplest kind of limit is one which is constant. However, it is also conceivable that the momentary capacity of the system changes, within finite and, in principle, measurable limits. The capacity might be altered by the nature of the task, motivational factors like the importance of the task, and organismic factors including blood alcohol level or fatigue. Single channel theory does not explicitly require that the capacity limitation be fixed, but it tends to be interpreted to mean that the capacity is invariant for a given task performance by a notionally standard subject. This particular aspect of the single channel hypothesis has not been the focus of much discussion so far, perhaps because the more central features of the hypothesis have been the subject of direct attack.

In this chapter we seek to present the main sources of evidence that lead to the single channel view and some of the discrepancies that have been discovered. We shall also try to indicate ways in which the basic view may need modification.

The major strength of the single channel hypothesis derives from the fact that it appears to account for data from diverse areas of enquiry and thereby to unify those areas. There are four main ones. These areas are choice amongst a limited set of alternatives, the control of movements, responding to successively presented stimuli and responding to more than one source of information.

The case for the single channel hypothesis

Choice amongst alternative responses

In Chapter 2 we introduced a discussion of the mechanism and processes which underlie performance when subjects are required to choose from amongst a predetermined set of responses. There are two main streams of evidence. One concerns the way in which reaction time increases as the number of alternative responses increases. This is Hick's Law. The other concerns the effect of varying the number of implicit comparisons the subject has to make internally before deciding between just two responses such as 'yes' or 'no'. This is essentially the task that Sternberg has explored.

The elegance of Hick's Law hinges on the discovery that the non-linear increase in reaction time as a function of the number of alternative responses can be turned into a straight line function. That is, reaction time is a linear function of the logarithm of the number of alternatives. This quantity can be used to specify the number of decisions that would have to be made, supposing that the set of alternatives was halved on each successive component decision. This interpretation lends support to the notion that reaction time is determined by the number of component decisions that have to be taken. If the set of alternatives is large more decisions are necessary than if the set is small. Making component decisions serially is congruent with the single channel view and the capacity limitation would be in terms of the time taken to make a decision.

The studies reviewed in Chapter 3 do not point unequivocally to a successive halving principle as the process underlying Hick's Law. Even Hick in his original paper pointed to the inadequacy of that scheme as an explanation of his own data. Subsequently other models of the underlying processes have been erected including those, such as Theios', which propose somewhat simpler linear searches through sets of ordered alternatives. However, most of these models incorporate some kind of serial search process and it is the serial character of this search which is critical. For if searches proceed serially that is support for the single channel view. Only one thing is being done at a time.

Though also concerned with reaction times and also dependent upon searching amongst a set, the Sternberg paradigm offers a different kind of support. The essential feature of his experiment is that the choice of response is always a choice between two responses. The subject is given a set of items. A further item then has to be classified as belonging to that set or not. As we saw in Chapter 2, data imply that subjects perform the task by searching through the memory set taking each item in it one at a time. The search proceeds serially. In so far as it does, performance on this task also offers support for the single channel hypothesis.

Controlling voluntary movements
The last three chapters have been devoted to the consideration of voluntary movements aimed towards a target and which have to be made with precision. Two particular aspects of that discussion are particularly relevant to the single channel issue. One concerns the nature of the processes which give rise to the relation between the speed and accuracy of movements, known

as Fitts' Law. The other concerns the pattern of corrections which characterizes subjects' attempts to track a continuously moving target.

We have seen that Fitts' Law provides a satisfactory numerically specified relation between the time taken to make a movement, the extent of that movement and the accuracy achieved. Movement time increases as a logarithmic function of the ratio of amplitude to accuracy. Once again, as for Hick's Law, the interpretation of this relation has been far from straightforward. The most promising view is that subjects specify a motor programme to make the aiming movement, and then correct it during the execution of the movement. The more accurate the movement is required to be, the greater the number of corrections that are necessary to achieve that accuracy. A satisfactory simulation of human performance is obtained by assuming that subjects make these corrections intermittently at intervals of a quarter of a second. The essential feature of this story is that the corrections are implemented intermittently rather than continuously. It is as if the underlying mechanisms take time to compute each correction, and each new correction has to wait until the computational mechanism has finished with the last.

Responding to successive stimuli

The third source of support for the single channel view comes from experiments that were stimulated by Vince's observations if intermittency in compensatory tracking (see p. 90). These experiments are concerned with the psychological refractory period. The experiments developed over a period of twenty years and were initially concerned to examine more closely what happens if a new stimulus in a reaction time experiment is presented very soon after a previous one. The intermittency which characterizes continuous tracking tasks would seem to predict that if the second stimulus arrives before the first one has been dealt with, it will have to wait. Furthermore, the sooner the second stimulus arrives, the longer it will have to wait.

This basic relation was verified in sundry experiments using both simple and choice reaction time tasks. A number of different theories have been advanced to account for the data (Smith, 1967). However, the single channel view, though a firm favourite with many researchers for some years, was not subjected to a direct test until 1967 in an experiment reported by Broadbent and Gregory.

There is one feature of this experiment which makes it outstanding. It tested directly the principal prediction from the single channel hypothesis, which is that the second arriving problem will have to wait until the computational channel is free before it can be processed. Broadbent and Gregory manipulated the difficulty of the first problem, and hence altered the time taken for a solution to it to be computed. Perhaps a concrete example will help to clarify this strategy. Consider a doctor's surgery. A patient goes into the consulting-room. Soon afterwards another patient arrives but he has to wait until the doctor has com-

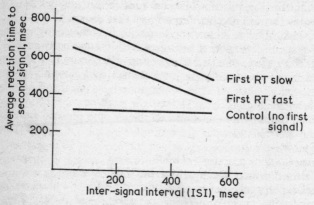

Fig. 7.1 *Effect of inter-signal interval and length of reaction time to first signal on reaction time to second signal. When the first RT is fast it occupies the channel for a short time and the second signal is delayed briefly. A slow first RT delays the second signal longer* (after Broadbent and Gregory, 1967).

pleted his consultation with the first patient. If the consultation takes ten minutes and the second patient arrives five minutes after the first patient goes into the doctor, he has to wait five minutes. However if the consultation takes longer, assuming a more difficult medical problem, say fifteen minutes, the second patient, arriving at the same time as before, now has to wait ten minutes. The time for which the second patient has to wait is also determined by how soon he arrives before the first patient's consultation is completed. If he arrives five minutes before the first patient leaves, he waits five minutes, if he arrives five minutes earlier than that, he waits ten, and so on.

The basic data from many experiments on the psychological refractory period conform in general terms to this model. The main step forward that Broadbent and Gregory made was to vary the processing time necessary to deal with the first stimulus. This is equivalent to manipulating the length of the consultation given to the first patient in the analogy above. The predictions were confirmed as shown in Figure 7.1.

Responding to simultaneous inputs

The last source of evidence for single-channel functioning comes from experiments usually considered under the heading of selective attention. These experiments are discussed in Chapter 6 in A4. Most of these experiments involve presenting two or more defined streams of information to a subject. The experimenter is then interested either in the degree to which there is interference between them or in the extent to which selective concentration on one leads to other sources being rejected. In nearly all experiments of this kind it is found that subjects required to deal with one stream of information extract very little from any simultaneous streams. The classic paradigm is the 'shadowing' experiment, in which subjects have to repeat orally a message heard in one ear while another message is presented to the other ear. Much of the evidence implies that the non-attended message is processed in a different way from the attended message. For example, the subject may not even notice the language of the unattended message.

Many experiments have been devised to explore the selectivity of attention and, in particular, to distinguish between the different theoretical views advanced by Broadbent (1958), Treisman (1964) and Deutsch and Deutsch (1963). These theories are concerned with the way in which selective attention as a phenomenon may be accounted for in terms of underlying processes. The original view postulated by Broadbent was that perception depended upon information being presented to a particular mechanism which analysed it in whatever way necessary for the development of a percept. However, the organism is bombarded by stimulation from all sides and it is necessary for the plethora of information to be filtered so that only signals relating to the chosen message are processed. Broadbent conceived of this filter as being like a switch with an all-or-none character. The selection of one source of information rather than another was considered to be in terms of the physical characteristics of the message such as its point of origin, or its principal sound frequencies and so on.

Though the nature of the processes underlying the complex phenomena of selective attention is far from clear, that does not matter for our argument in this chapter. This is because all theorists seeking to give an account of selective attention either specify somewhere in the system a mechanism with the characteristics of a single channel of limited capacity, or incorporate the concept implicitly. There is near universal acceptance of the idea that in an instant (however long that is supposed to be) the subject can only concentrate upon one kind of information. He can only 'think' about one thing at a time.

It might reasonably be asked how subjects give the illusion of doing several things at once. The one-man band would appear to be a dramatic example of this. The busker plays a mouth-organ, a drum, the cymbals and an accordion – all at once. If this is not an example of multi-channel processing, what is it? The single channel view would seem to be somewhat stretched to account for this kind of behaviour. However, if these several aspects of behaviour are very well learned it is possible to imagine that the processing necessary to monitor them imposes a relatively light load and that satisfactory control could be effected by switching the monitoring and control system from task to task in rapid succession. In fact only one task would be under control at a time, but because the others would be free-running, defined only by the previously specified motor programme, the illusion of multi-channel processing would be given. We shall see in Chapter 9 that perhaps one of the alternatives to strict single channel operation offers a more plausible explanation.

The defence rests

In summary, then, several different sources of evidence have been seen to point towards the single channel hypothesis. This wide applicability is one of the reasons that single channel theory has received continuing acclaim. However, twenty years of research have not proved enough to establish the hypothesis beyond doubt, nor to do very much to fill out the details of its operation. The hypothesis does little more than assert that somewhere in the chain of processes between input and output one or more processes act in this single channel manner. It does not say that all have to. It does say that the 'weakest link' in that chain will be a single channel process and this puts upper limits on the performance of the system overall.

The case against, and cross-examination

Practice effects and number of alternatives

Evidence that Hick's Law is not universal was found in the experiment of Leonard (1959) and Mowbray and Rhoades (1959), discussed in Chapter 3. The absence in these two cases of the usual sloping RT function is awkward for a limited capacity model (unless it has multiple channels) because such horizontal RT functions may imply an infinitely high rate of information processing.

Mowbray and Rhoades practised their subjects over a long period on a two-stimulus and four-stimulus condition in which the stimuli in the smaller set were included in the larger. But this inclusiveness may be crucial, since if the subject always treated the situation as relating to the larger set of alternatives then no effect of the number of alternatives would be expected. Mowbray was aware of this and in 1960 reported an experiment in which different subjects served at each set size, and again there was no sign of the Hick effect. But there is a snag here as well since digits were used as stimuli and unfamiliar subsets (e.g. four and eight in the two-choice condition) were used. So the same problem that the subject may have responded as if a larger number of choices applied (e.g. all the digits) bedevilled this experiment too.

The inclusiveness argument could also be made against the Leonard study. It will be remembered from Chapter 3 that the stimuli in this experiment were tactual vibrations applied to the fingers. In fact the subjects used were 'unfamiliar' here too. A more popular counter-argument is that the response to this kind of stimulus is almost reflex-like, and it may be capable of being organized and selected at a quite low level in the brain.

A second attack on the single channel question comes through some work on visual search by Neisser (1963), considered in more detail in Chapter 8 of A4. Neisser found that, with something like twenty to thirty days of practice, searching for any one of ten alternatives took no longer than searching for one. This suggests that up to ten channels can be simultaneously active. However, Neisser in 1967 discussed such effects in terms of a multiple channel system located pre-attentively, that is prior to the single channel of selective attention. The single channel hypothesis escapes the axe again.

The study of practice effects is of particular interest because although it cannot entirely protect the experiments from the charge of artificiality, it does serve to shift them in the direction of a set of circumstances that seem to apply to the exercise of everyday skills. This evidence seems on balance not to require a radical deviation from a single channel position.

Psychological refractory period

Back in the doctor's waiting-room for a moment, it will be noted that the amount of time by which the second patient is delayed can be as much as the time taken to deal with the first patient (if they both arrive together) or nothing at all (if the second arrives just as the first leaves). The delay otherwise depends on the difference in their arrival times.

The bigger the difference, the shorter the delay. We can show this diagrammatically as in Figure 7.2. The 'time in surgery' for the second patient decreases uniformly, one minute less for every minute added to the difference in their arrival times.

This unit-for-unit decrease is an important prediction for the single channel hypothesis and is known as the unit negative slope prediction. It has only very rarely been confirmed. Experiments typically report gentler slopes, as if the delay is usefully spent by the doctor getting some information about the second patient so his consultation time effectively begins before the first man leaves.

The two most serious problems for the single channel hypothesis are the failure to observe the unit negative slope and the existence of some data that imply that the *nature* of the second task and its time of arrival influence the latency of the first response.

Referring again to the doctor's surgery situation, it can be seen that there is no reason why the impending arrival of the second patient, or his presence in the waiting-room or his time of arrival should influence the time taken to deal with the first. Unless of course the doctor himself is also responsible for opening the door to patients, or the patient makes a distracting fuss in the waiting-room. Nor should the second patient's identity make a difference to how long the doctor takes in treating the first, unless the doctor on noticing the man's name on the appointments list starts anticipating how to deal with his case. And yet effects like these have been regularly reported in the psychological refractory period literature.

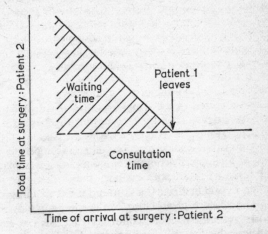

Fig. 7.2 *Doctor's surgery model of psychological refractory period. Patient 2 may arrive before patient 1 has left. If he does he will have to wait. The earlier he arrives the longer he waits, and for every minute earlier he arrives he waits another minute. This relation is called the unit negative slope function.*

It has long been recognized that the time of arrival of the second signal can be crucial for how the first is handled. If it is brief enough then the subject may adopt a strategy of 'grouping' the two signals and making a coordinated pair of responses to them. Then the RT to the first signal is liable to reflect the interval between the signals. The effect of a 'grouping' strategy would be to delay the processing of the first signal until the second had arrived. This would be like a joint consultation with the doctor. In this way evidence that RT to the first signal depends on the time of arrival of the second signal can frequently be accommodated by a single channel account with a grouping

103

principle as 'longstop'. A precise quantitative model would be necessary to take this much further.

Perhaps the most significant findings against single channel theory came from a series of elegant studies of stimulus-response compatibility factors in the psychological refractory period paradigm. These experiments extend and qualify the findings of Broadbent and Gregory (1967) discussed above. Way and Gottsdanker (1968) found that the response to the first signal was slower if the second response had to be made in the *opposite direction*, even though the movement required in both cases was compatible with the stimulus to which it was made. It appears therefore that compatibility between the tasks is important (see p. 38). The critical aspect of these data, however, is that they imply that the *nature* of the second response can affect the latency of the first response.

This is supported in the strongest terms by further findings reported by Triggs (1968). He compared the performance of independent groups of subjects when the second task was either a compatible choice reaction, or an incompatible choice reaction, or a simple reaction. Strong emphasis was placed on the first response in order to establish the priority for channel occupation by the first signal and in order to rule out grouping effects. The absence of an effect of the inter-stimulus interval on the first response latencies confirmed that this was effective. Nevertheless the first RT was affected by the *nature* of the second task. Relative to a control condition where there was no second task, it was least delayed when the second task was a simple reaction, and it was most delayed when one of the tasks was compatible and the other incompatible (i.e. there was a change of mapping rule between the two tasks). These results suggest, at the least, that the *expected* arrival of the second signal alters the manner in which the first is processed and, at most, that the two signals are processed in some interactive fashion. Whichever of these alternatives is preferred, some modification of the simple doctor's surgery view of the single channel operation will be required.

So far a totally satisfactory alternative has not been discovered. Triggs (1968) supported the idea of a limited capacity system which could be allocated between tasks. If the proportion of available capacity were allocated to each expected task *in advance* of the first stimulus arriving, and if the basis for the allocation were determined by the expected difficulty and importance of each task, many of the phenomena which seem to embarrass the strict single channel hypothesis could be accommodated. In order to predict a constant response latency to the first stimulus, and a non-unit negative slope for the second response latency, the only further assumption that is needed is that the full processing capacity is switched to the second task as soon as the first is completed. The effect of the complexity of the second task on the latency of the first response is attributable to the allocation of capacity in anticipation of the relative degree of difficulty of the two tasks.

In fact, it makes no difference to this 'divisible capacity' hypothesis, whether the capacity is shared between processes operating in parallel or a time-sharing system is operated. If it is time-sharing the single channel can be conceived of as being switched between the two tasks. However, it would require this vacillation to occur even before the arrival of the second signal; perhaps the system constantly watches for its appearance. The great virtue of the time-sharing interpretation is that the single channel concept can be retained – what goes is the idea that signals are processed to the point of defining responses in *one* uninterrupted computation.

Mathematical analysis of the effects of time of arrival of a second stimulus reveals counter-intuitively that if time-sharing is restricted to the period of overlap of the two tasks, *unit* negative slopes are predicted. Such slopes are reported, for instance, by Herman and McCauley (1969). It appears that the key to *non*-unit negative slopes is the operation of a time-sharing (or equivalent capacity sharing) mechanism *prior* to the arrival of the second signal. In addition, the deviation from a unit negative slope will be determined by the relative amounts of processing time allocated to the two tasks. The higher the proportion devoted to the first signal the closer the approximation to a unit negative slope.

At present it seems that a rescue of the single channel hypothesis is quite possible, though its salvation depends upon conceiving of reaction time tasks as comprising a series of processing steps. Such a radical conceptual change opens the way for all sorts of interactive influences without compromising the single channel operation of the computational mechanisms.

Doing two things at once

According to single channel theory the performance of two tasks at the same time is either impossible, or only achievable if their demands can be met by a rapid alternation of attention between them. The essence of this is that the single channel can only ever be devoted to processing operations called for by one task at a time. In any event the reasoning is that if two tasks have to be done at once then performance of both will suffer. The data of experience are generally marshalled at this point to show that two things are habitually done at the same time (conversing while driving, knitting while watching television, and so on). But they are not a very good guide as we see by the lapse in conversation when negotiating a tricky set of circumstances in driving, and the dropped stitch at a point of high TV drama.

Clearly it is essential that the question be put on a formal basis. There is plenty of evidence that dual-task situations do lead to impairment of the performance of both tasks – and the research on selective attention and the psychological refractory period amply demonstrates this. But as observed by Allport, Antonis and Reynolds (1972) the two tasks are usually very similar if not identical. So the subject might be asked to shadow (cf. p. 99) one of two spoken messages, or he might have to organize manual responses to a pair of stimuli so scheduled that the response to the first is still ongoing when the second stimulus arrives. What happens if the tasks are dissimilar?

Allport *et al.* chose shadowing as one task because it is, on the evidence, 'the paradigm of tasks requiring complete and uninterrupted occupation of the hypothetical single channel'. The second task varied. In one experiment the second task was to memorize auditory verbal, visual verbal or pictorial stimuli. The to-be-remembered auditory material was presented to the ear not receiving the shadowing message. In this condition performance was at a chance level, agreeing with previous evidence. But performance on the other two memory tasks, notably picture recognition, although below the level of an undivided-attention control condition, was much better. According to single channel theory modality ought not to matter if the shadowing task is in full possession of the channel, no material therefore should be remembered. Even a time-sharing amendment would not cope since the switching between tasks ought to be possible in all cases.

In a second study Allport *et al.* combined shadowing with the task of sight-reading piano music. Both tasks were also done under conditions of undivided attention. The results were remarkable. Sight-reading was quite unaffected by simultaneous shadowing, and there was virtually no effect on efficiency of shadowing either. Close examination of the timing of the shadowing responses suggested that time-sharing had not occurred, since there were no signs of an increase in the number of gaps and speech bursts in the divided attention condition.

To account for these findings Allport *et al.* suggested that a multi-channel model was needed. Performance of a complex task is achieved by a battery of independent parallel processors, possibly individually characterized by a single-channel mode of operation. These processors may be called on by two different, but similar, tasks and the extent to which they are needed will be reflected by mutual interference in the performance of them. Sufficiently different tasks may not involve common processors and in this event will not show reciprocal effects in dual-task conditions.

A further examination of subjects' abilities to do two things at once has been reported by Shaffer (1975). He ran a series of experiments on one very highly skilled typist using a special keyboard that input directly to a computer. In this way very detailed analysis of inter-response times and error patterns could be made. The quite extraordinary results were that she could copy-type visually presented material as well when shadowing auditorially presented prose as she could without the shadowing task. While these two tasks differ in terms of input modality and output mode they would be expected to share a common linguistic system of some kind. The key to this 'virtuoso' performance probably lies in her very high level of typing skill. She maintained a typing-speed of about 100 words per minute, with or without the second task. Further experiments revealed that she had greater difficulty when the tasks were reversed and she had to shadow visually presented material. She also had difficulty in audio-typing while reciting. Shaffer suggests that the principal difficulty may be in trying to speak and listen at the same time. The same modality then has to serve two different monitoring functions, and does so rather poorly. These results lend additional weight to Allport's and point once again to the possibility of multiple parallel processing channels. This evidence seems exceedingly difficult to encompass within an unmodified strict single channel model.

Our preference is for a multi-channel processing system comprising a super-ordinate single channel to which a processing problem may be referred if necessary, and a collection of subordinate special-purpose parallel channels. These latter are programmed to deal with the detailed and menial calculations required by most tasks most of the time. When skills have been learned sufficiently to become 'automatic' it is because these subordinate channels have been established. This speculative view of information processing is elaborated further in Chapter 9.

Summary

The progress of the single channel hypothesis has been like that of an old drunk lurching his way home, every minute in danger of falling flat on his face but ever finding a conveniently placed lamp-post, passer-by or whatever for support. Close inspection reveals that he is in fact an honourable, tax-paying, up-standing member of the community who has an honest job of work to do but its demands on him are excessive. It remains to be seen whether he will fail to get home one evening, or whether he will be retired first. Our bet is that top management will see to it that he is gracefully pensioned off and replaced by a team of whizz-kids one of whom will be delegated the old man's job.

8
Practice makes perfect

Fifty years ago it was most unlikely that an author considering the problem of learning would delimit the nature of what was learned. He would draw on the findings of human and animal research concerning the learning of any kind of behaviour. Nowadays the field has become more specialized and research on, for example, human verbal learning (see A6) has less in common with the sort of learning research for which non-human subjects are preferred. This is partly because the hypotheses which experimenters seek to test have become more specific and task dependent, and partly because there is a growing belief that a single theory will not be sufficient to accommodate all of the varieties of experience-produced alterations in behaviour. This chapter is concerned with the acquisition of perceptual-motor skills.

A preliminary consideration of learning different kinds of 'new' behaviour indicates that very often a new perceptual-motor skill bears considerable resemblance to an already learned one. The difference between old and new seems rather less dramatic than in learning a new complex visual discrimination, or a new list of words. What this is saying is that new skills are often based upon old ones. Learning to drive a car utilizes the well-practised skills of placing and aiming, and learning to drive another car benefits considerably from the initial driving tuition.

This chapter will be restricted to a number of issues surrounding adults when they learn skills, and assumes that basic movement control processes exist upon which new skills can be erected. The sorts of skills considered are also restricted. One can imagine an almost limitless range of distinguishable skills, from driving a grand prix racing car to writing one's signature. However, skills can be meaningfully divided into two categories: those which are basically movements of short duration, though perhaps executed with great accuracy, and those which entail a sequence of movements making up a complex action. A golf-swing would be an example of the former, a signature of the latter.

The title of this chapter is not literally true. Perfection is probably unattainable. There have been a number of studies of skilled performance extending over long periods of practice. One of the longest is documented by Crossman (1959). He reports the speed of performance of women operating cigar-making machines. Even after making ten million cigars over a period of about seven years the women were still showing continued improvements in skill. Of course, the rate of improvement slows down as skill increases but it does not appear to reach a ceiling. It raises the question whether motivation may not be as important a determiner of the ultimate level of skill acquired as some more mechanistic attribute of the information-processing system.

The cigar-makers showed continuing improvement as a function of practice as distinct from training. Training implies that circumstances are arranged to produce the most rapid improvement in skill possible (see E3). This usually means that a coach or tutor will guide and correct the trainee. During practice no such helpful outside influence exists. Improvement as a result of training is, perhaps, not too surprising, but improvement just as a result of practice seems a little more mysterious. Any successful theory of skill learning must obviously provide an account of how training produces improvements and also how, after the initial stages of learning have been mastered, sheer practice is sufficient to produce further improvements.

Factors conducive to skill learning

There seem to be two mainstays of successful training schemes. These are guidance and feedback. They are discussed in an excellent and readable book by Holding (1965) (see too E3).

The essential difference between these two factors is that guidance in some way tells the trainee what to do while feedback tells him how successful he has been.

Guidance
Guidance can take many forms ranging from the physical imposition upon the subject of the movements that have to be learned, to a verbal description of what to do. For example, it is argued that in order to play golf well a reliable swing is a *sine qua non*. Acquiring one is the subject of the expenditure of money, time and energy. One training aid that could be used is a machine that moves a golf-club through the desired arc while the would-be amateur open champion hangs onto the handle. The machine does all the work and the trainee plays a relatively passive role. He can learn what the swing should feel like in terms of both the shape of the arc the club should make through the air and its timing. This is active physical guidance.

Passive guidance can also be provided. The main difference is that the trainee does the work. For instance, a harness of wires can be arranged to constrain the movement of the golf-club through the desired arc but the horse-power to make it move at all comes from the player. This arrangement clearly requires a more active participation on the part of the trainee but the apparatus still prevents him from making errors.

Verbal instructions either about how to perform in a psychological experiment, or how to drive a car or play golf are the most common form of guidance used in skill training. They are usually used to convey two kinds of information: what the objectives are and how to reach them. Words can be very valuable in defining objectives but they are much less useful in conveying methods of achieving them.

This difference leads to direct and indirect uses of verbal guidance. Instructions about how to shift from one gear to another can be given without difficulty. They consist of a series of sub-goals such as depression of the clutch pedal, grasping the gear-shift knob, moving it to a new position and so on. The instructions do not say how each sub-goal is to be reached. They do not tell the learner how to make the required movements. He has to discover that for himself, building on his past experience and previously acquired skills. However, the situation is different when there are few such skills to draw on or when they do not relate directly to the new situation. Miller, Galanter and Pribram (1960) discuss the problem of teaching a skier to make a turn. They suggest that in order to encourage him to adopt the posture which brings the turn about he should be instructed to imagine putting one hand across the front of his body and into the opposite trouser pocket. The purpose of this instruction is to attempt to bring about a postural change similar to the one required. It can be achieved by specifying sub-goals that bear no relation whatsover to skiing but happen to involve a movement pattern similar to the one required. Verbal guidance is limited to specifying perceptible sub-goals either relating directly to the task in hand, or producing appropriate movements as a by-product.

Feedback

The other main factor in training is feedback. This is often called 'knowledge of results' (KR), especially when it is provided intermittently as a summary of performance, such as a final score. Holding (1965) itemizes the various forms that feedback and knowledge of results can take. The principal bases of classification are whether it is artificial or intrinsic, verbal or non-verbal, accumulated and terminal or separate and concurrent.

Intrinsic feedback is information that is a natural feature of the task. It is contrasted with artificial feedback which is provided only during the training regimen and is sometimes called augmented feedback because it is added to the intrinsic feedback. Intrinsic feedback will be available to help guide performance after the training period is over, augmented feedback will not. Annett (1969) concludes that augmented feedback can often produce a considerable improvement in performance if it is concurrent and therefore gives an immediate indication to the learner about his accuracy. However, as soon as it is removed performance declines dramatically. So much so, that in many instances it is better for the augmented feedback never to have been given. What seems to happen is that the learner comes to rely upon the obviously salient augmented feedback and fails to learn the more subtle cues to performance that the task provides intrinsically.

Apart from these main classifications of feedback one of its most important features is its precision. In a blind aiming task, the subject may be told that he hit or missed the target, overshot or undershot, or made an error of +5·2 cm. These represent various degrees of precision of verbal feedback but equivalent information could be signalled non-verbally. As might be imagined performance improves more rapidly when more detailed feedback is given. Being told that he missed provides a poor basis for doing better next time, whereas a quantitative measure of his error allows him to compute a graduated correction, at least in theory.

Theories of skill learning

Guidance and feedback are two of the biggest guns in the coach's training armoury. Efficiently deployed they work very well and substantially reduce the time it takes to reach a given level of proficiency. We can now consider what is supposed to have happened to the underlying mechanisms during training and see how performance changes.

Stimulus-response theories

The essence of stimulus-response (S-R) theories is that responses become attached to stimuli, so that occurrence of the stimulus is a sufficient condition for emission of the response (see A3). Exactly how this happens remains a mystery. Simple models on the lines of a telephone connection seem to be implied. When a particular number is dialled, a particular telephone rings. The initial attraction of these kinds of theory was that only observable entities were involved.

However, the key feature of skill is its adaptive nature and its characteristic of adjustment to the demands of a situation and to achieve defined goals. The goal-directedness of skill would appear to be poorly described by stimulus driven S-R theories.

It is undeniably true that skilled behaviour cannot be accounted for in terms of learning specific responses to specific stimuli. If it were, an efficient, accurate movement could only be made if, in the past, the same stimulus conditions had prevailed and a positively reinforced response made to them. The criticism that Chomsky (1959) levelled at Skinner's (1957) account of language acquisition in terms of S-R associations (see A7) can be applied here too. The rich variety of satisfactory perceptual-motor performance even in a child would require many lifetimes to acquire in that way. As with language (or at least its syntax), rules are acquired rather than specific connections between stimuli and responses.

Whether S-R theory can offer a satisfactory account of rule learning is debatable. What is clear is that an S-R account of tracking would be a very complex one because its units of analysis are so microscopic. Principles like error-correction would entail a vast list of contingent-specific S-R routes amongst many levels of internal (and thus hypothetical) responses and stimuli. It may well be the case that an accurate S-R model of the underlying mechanisms could be assembled. But even if it were it is doubtful whether it would be useful. Its very complexity would make it unmanageable as a basis for predicting performance, and thus an unconvincing model. The units of analysis are too small and the level of discourse too elementary. For these reasons the language and concepts of cybernetics (see p. 69) have been preferred. The units there are in terms of functions and the specification of the overall model is never far out of sight. The wood of cybernetics is a more comfortable theoretical basis than the trees of S-R associations.

Notwithstanding speculations about the ultimate resource-fulness of S-R theorists seeking to transmute feedback theory into their own terms, the classical stimulus-response account of sequences of responses which form a coordinated action pattern is in terms of simple S-R chains. Each response gives rise to a stimulus to which another response is made. The response-produced stimulus is, of course, feedback by another name. So this kind of theory is one which asserts that skill is governed by continuous feedback.

Perhaps the most influential attack on this view was made by Lashley (1951). His analytical criticism was supported by Keele (1968) and Adams (1971), who cite further evidence that response sequences involve too little time for each component to act as a stimulus for the next, and considerable evidence from animal experimentation, which implies a less than crucial role for proprioception in the control of well-learned movements.

The radical alternative to S-R chaining is the motor programme. Since the S-R model involves feedback it is sometimes called a closed-loop model, using the language of cybernetics. In contrast motor programme theory is strictly an open-loop model. (An open-loop system does not respond to the feedback

114

from its operation.) The theory is developed from the concept of the motor programme, or implicit response described earlier, as an essential basis for making simple movements. The theory takes this basic notion and gives the motor programme the role of determining not just a single movement but a series of movements.

Open-loop operation made possible by the existence of a motor programme would certainly permit the control of behaviour in the absence of relevant feedback. This kind of explanation seems apposite for the musician's arpeggio and the complex behaviour produced by animals whose sensory input channels have been interfered with. It also provides a basis for Poulton's (1957) subject, who went on tracking a sine-wave for five seconds after the lights had been unexpectedly extinguished. However, open-loop control, while it may be efficient for some purposes when the task demands are predictable, as they are in driving from the golf tee or signing one's name, has a major deficiency. It is inflexible in operation and cannot be adjusted to correct for any errors in its execution or changes in the situation. There is also a major problem in specifying how an extended motor programme is assembled in the first place.

Adams' closed-loop theory

An elegant solution to the problems evident in an exclusive application either of continuous response-produced stimulus control of actions or of open-loop motor programme control has been advanced by Adams (1971). His theory is usually called a closed-loop theory but the way in which the loop is closed alters as skill improves and as the to-be-learned sequence of movements becomes more familiar. In many ways it resembles a mixture of the earlier theories since movements are postulated initially to be under closed-loop control and subsequently the motor programme established in that way takes over. Other important changes in control are also essential features of this theory.

One of the key concepts in this theory is the distinction between verbal-motor control of performance early in learning and motor control which takes over later. This reflects the value of verbal guidance during initial training when verbal instructions form the basis of the developing skill. Again let us consider learning to drive. For the first few hours of tuition the learner may use his tutor's words to organize what to do and when. The linguistic version of the skill is initially dominant.

Adams conceptualizes this stage as one during which verbal instructions may be used to define sub-goals and preliminary objectives. Knowledge of results from the task is evaluated against these sub-goals and, with continued training, a motor programme for this particular performance is assembled and stored in memory. The use of knowledge of results clearly establishes the closed-loop features of learning during this stage. However, as the long-range motor programme is being assembled a template, or ideal pattern, is also being established against which intrinsic feedback can be evaluated. During this early phase in learning, it is argued that verbal knowledge of results or its equivalent is a prerequisite for improvement in performance. Feedback, and, in particular, proprioceptive and tactual feedback, is considered uninterpretable as a basis for evaluating performance. However, the establishment of a feedback template makes continued knowledge of results irrelevant since intrinsic feedback from making particular responses can be evaluated directly. As a consequence further improvement can occur in the absence of verbal knowledge of results since proprioceptive feedback can now perform an equivalent function. In this way after sufficient *training*, pure *practice* can lead to further improvement in skill.

This theory, therefore, combines the most useful features of S-R chain association theory and pure motor programme theory. Feedback fulfils a monitoring function which is the basis for the operation of an error detection and correction process. This monitoring function of feedback is what Bartlett (1947) considered to be the essence of skill in contrast to habit. The actual sequencing of component movements, however, is controlled directly by a motor programme rather than being determined inflexibly by the feedback itself. In this way the theory accounts for behaviour in the absence of feedback as well as the flexible modification of behaviour when feedback indicates that the ongoing sequence is not satisfactory. It also shows how training, with its provision of augmented feedback (verbal knowledge of results), sets the scene for the later stage of skill acquisition when, after the feedback evaluation template has been established, pure practice can lead to further improvement on the basis of intrinsic feedback alone.

Improvements in performance could result simply by doing the same things as were done at an earlier stage of practice but doing them more efficiently. For example, movements could be completed more quickly, with greater accuracy and with the consequently reduced probability of having to implement a correction. The coordination of movements could also be improved by controlling the timing of responses more precisely. If this happened a quantitative improvement would be observed but no qualitative change would have occurred. However, there have been many reports of qualitative changes in the processes underlying the control of skilled performances. Several different sorts of change have been postulated. Two principal ones will be mentioned here.

The changing information base of skill

We have already discussed how verbal instructions and knowledge of results dominate at the beginning of many training courses (see E3). However, as training continues these become decreasingly important until eventually performance can be not only maintained on the basis of intrinsic feedback alone, but actually improved further simply as a result of continued practice. This initial dependence upon verbal information giving way to task-produced non-verbal and often proprioceptive information was recognized by James (1890). Adams (1971) constructed an explicit theory of skill learning in which this change in the basis of performance forms an essential part. Along with this decreased dependence on verbal instruction and knowledge of results goes a decreased consciousness of the control of the movements comprising the total task. For instance, to the learner driver shifting gear is a major hurdle requiring deliberate attention to clutch, gear-stick, steering-wheel, gas-pedal and so on. He may also be rehearsing a verbal formula designed to guide him in the skill, so that he makes the various movements in the right order and at the right time. Before long, however, he will find the deliberation which characterized his earlier performance reduces until the skilled driver reaches the point of changing gear in response to the demands of the road and traffic conditions without noticing that he does so. He may very well have to look to see which gear he is in! In this sense of having been removed from verbal (and conscious) control the gear-shifting skill has become automatic.

Other changes in the ways in which movements are controlled may also occur. The change from verbal to non-verbal control is mirrored in the change from visual to proprioceptive control inferred by Fleishman and Rich (1963). They showed that performance on a complex multiple tracking task, simulating some aspects of flying an aircraft, was heavily dependent upon subjects' visuo-spatial abilities early in training. However, as training proceeded proprioceptive abilities became increasingly important. This change is also congruent with the changed mode of operation which is the core of Adams' theory.

Changes in the organization of skill

In addition to changes in the information used to monitor performance, there are changes in the organization of performance as practice continues. These changes are mainly alterations in the functional units of skill. In short, as skill increases the sequences of movements which are controlled as units increase in size. Back to the learner driver again, he makes separate clutch-depression, accelerator release, gear-shift movements and so on until he is once more in gear. The skilled driver carries out the total sequence as a single coordinated action pattern.

Comparable changes are found in transcription skills such as typewriting. Initially the would-be typist proceeds letter by letter. Gradually some of the more common two-letter combinations are typed as 'a unit' until eventually some whole words may be produced in this way. The classic work on this topic is by Bryan and Harter (1899), and their account of the progressive increase in complexity of the functional units of performance stands as firmly today as ever it did. However, they also asserted that performance improves discontinuously so that plateaux interrupt the smooth progress of improving performance. These plateaux were supposed to represent a period when the skill was in the process of reorganization. The claim was not made generally but only for the skill of receiving morse code. Unfortunately it seems that, though distinctly plausible, they were mistaken. Keller (1959) reviews several attempts to replicate these claims and concludes that they are in fact phantoms. However, the general claim that the changes occur is not questioned.

Considering tracking rather than the complex serial response skill of transcription, it is possible to give an account of the detailed operation of the mechanisms underlying performance. A particularly elegant analysis was reported by Fuchs (1962). He constructed a mathematical model of a subject performing a tracking task. The model was based upon cybernetic considerations and defined the relation of the output of the system to the tracking error in a compensatory tracking task. The equations took account of position, velocity and acceleration control, and the relative contribution of these different orders of control could be manipulated. (Briggs, 1964, refers to this mathematical function as a 'manalogue' model.) Fuchs then coupled a small computer programmed with the manalog function to a tracking task being performed by a real subject. Both subject and computer received the same error signals from the task and the manalog function was adjusted so that man and computer produced the same output. In fact, the man was unaware that control had been switched from him to the computer for periods as long as half a minute.

The point of this experiment was to discover how the man changed in his tracking performance as he continued to practise over a twenty-day period. This was inferred from the detailed values of the manalog equation which matched him in performance. The results indicate that the relative importance of position control declines with practice, while velocity and acceleration control assumes a correspondingly more important role. In other words, practice results in control migrating towards a higher order. We noted in Chapter 6 how this results in smoother tracking performance and may be, in principle, a more efficient mode of organization. It also represents in a continuous control task an increase in the 'size' of the units which govern performance. It is the direct analogue in a continuous control task of the development from letters to letter groups to words in transcription skills such as sending and receiving morse code and typewriting.

Rules and responses

We have seen how skill learning involves two primary features, the learning of a motor programme which is appropriate to the problem and the learning of a feedback template against which intrinsic performance feedback can be evaluated. However,

119

many skills cannot be performed simply by implementing a tried and tested programme. The situations in which these skills are required are too uncertain and the requirements of movements too unpredictable. Tracking an unpredictable (quasi-random) course is such a situation. What is required here is not a repertoire of motor programmes but a set of rules which will lead to the development of appropriate movements. These rules may relate to the way in which manipulation of the controls changes the performance of the system being controlled. Learning these rules is one of the problems in learning to use a complex control system. Steering a ship efficiently requires application of the rules governing the operation of a second-order control system. These rules are called the control system dynamics and learning them is probably part of what is meant by 'getting the feel of the controls'. It is what Poulton (1957) was referring to under the label effector anticipation. A successful motor programme cannot be assembled unless the consequences of its execution can be predicted.

Adams' closed-loop theory has been presented as if it could only deal with the problem of producing stereotyped responses such as driving a golf-ball and signing one's name. However, the same essential structure can also provide the basis for learning the relation between effector response and system response. This relation cannot be adequately specified in terms of a list of particular values of one variable which correspond to particular values of the other. A rule has to be found, not a list of equivalent values.

This discussion of the acquisition of skill has returned repeatedly to the problem of learning rules. Different sets of rules govern the determination of the required object modulation, the required effector modulation and the implicit response. Without these rules behaviour would exhibit haphazard trial-and-error features, which are the antithesis of skill. Discovery of how these rules are acquired and how they are applied in the performance of skills will be one of the most significant milestones in understanding skilled behaviour.

9
Plans, processes and perspectives

Our discussion of skills and the processes underlying them has ranged broadly. We have considered each of the main kinds of skilled behaviour: corrected and uncorrected responses, various sorts of tracking and the exercise of well-learned sequences of actions. Inevitably, we have been unable to develop these considerations in depth and sometimes controversial issues have been passed over at breakneck speed. Two main ideas have sustained us on our journey. These were a fairly simple model of the underlying processes (see p. 18) and the concept of single channel operation (see Ch. 7). In this chapter we shall elaborate these further, seeking to weave these threads together. To do so involves considerable speculation and goes beyond the point where data can be called upon for support. Perhaps these ideas will be looked upon in the future as wild aberrations; for the present, we find the conceptual structure they provide both helpful and stimulating.

The mark II model

In the version of the model outlined in Chapter 1 three basic processing stages were specified. These stages defined a set of changes in their outputs. They were changes to the environment involving an alteration to the subject-controlled object (that is the required object modulation, ROM), a set of coded instructions or motor programme which when expanded in time would act on the muscles and joints comprising the effector system (that is the implicit response, IR), and finally the actual set of signals sent along the efferent nerves to the muscles.

It is now apparent that a four-stage model would be more appropriate. The principal reason for identifying an additional stage comes from considering the strategies used in training people in new skills (see Ch. 8) and how subjects perform on simultaneously demanding tasks. It is also implied by the consequences of introducing a complex relation between what the subject does with his hands (or feet) and what happens to the object that he is required by the task to control. This new stage receives the ROM as its command (or reference) signal and determines the changes in the effector system necessary to achieve it. Its output is the required effector modulation (REM). The REM acts in turn as the command signal which determines the assembly of an implicit response. The remainder of the model continues unchanged.

The processing stages which are the essence of the model are summarized in Figure 9.1, which shows the principal inputs and outputs to and from each of the four stages.

Stage one. This stage is in reality many different stages and it is referred to as one stage only because, from the point of view of the processes underlying perceptual-motor skill, it can be so treated. It is the stage which determines what needs to be done in terms of manipulations of the environment, that is the ROM. In a target acquisition task this stage has to appraise the situation and define the change in the object necessary to meet the demands of the task. This will entail perceiving the relative locations of target and object. In one-dimensional acquisition and tracking tasks this operation is relatively straightforward, but this stage also subserves the decision to move one's pawn to Queen's Bishop 3. That may involve a far more complex piece of problem-solving.

Stage two. This is the key stage in the organization of skilled responses. It is here that the problem of how to bring about the required object modulation is solved by specifying changes in the effector system, the required effector modulation (REM). In addition to the ROM command signal, it requires informa-

122

	Stage one	Stage two	Stage three	Stage ?
Sensory input	Information about relative location within the world; particularly about target and object. All modalities but mainly visual.	Information about the spatial location of the various parts of the effector system, mainly provided by proprioception.	Detailed information about physical state of effectors; including prevailing muscle-tension and joint angles. Signalled by proprioception.	?
Command (reference) signal	Task demand: to match object to target.	Required object modulation (ROM).	Required effector modulation (REM).	Implicit response (IR).
Rules of operation	Task demands and (verbal) instructions. (Usually verbally applied in learning.)	Rules governing effect of responses on the object, control system dynamics. (May be verbally applied early in learning.)	Rules governing effect of muscular changes in the effectors they control, including the bases for motor constancy. (Non-verbal.)	?
Output	Required object modulation (ROM). Specification of the changes to the object necessary to meet task demands.	Required effector modulation (REM). Specification of changes to effector position and movement, necessary to produce desired effect on object.	Implicit response (IR) motor programme defining in a compactly coded form a sequence of muscular changes.	Efferent neural signal (ENS). Train of impulses down various motor (efferent) nerves changing the activity of the muscles to which they lead.

Fig. 9.1 Summary of the mark II model of the processes underlying the performance of skills. Stage three rules are thought to be less flexible in form than those governing the operation of Stages one and two. They are also likely to be 'wired in' to the system. The method of operation of Stage four is in many respects obscure. In general the operation of each stage is determined by the command (reference) signal and it operates so as to meet the demands of that signal.

123

tion about the effector system and a set of rules which enable an appropriate REM to be determined. The Hick-Hyman function and stimulus-response compatibility effects are both thought to arise from the operation of this processing stage.

The main set of rules governing its operation are the control system dynamics, a set of functions relating changes in the effector system to changes to the object which the effector system controls. In this sense S-R compatibility is a special case of control system dynamics and so a first cousin to a second-order (acceleration) control system like that involved in steering a car.

Stage three. On entry to this stage the system has defined what is to be done in terms of changes in the effector system, and this stage has the responsibility of determining the motor programme or implicit response which will bring that change about. The operating code has now changed completely from an input (sensory or perceptual) code to an output (motor) code which is one of the reasons why there is no conscious correlate of the activity involved in this stage. For example, one simply wills that one's hand should move. One specifies the movement in a conscious manner, but there is no impression of how the movement is achieved. It just happens.

The efficient operation of this stage also depends upon the availability of rules which will allow an appropriate implicit response to be assembled. These rules are the basis of effector anticipation and stipulate the relation between the implicit response and the effects of its implementation on the effector system. Part of these effector anticipation rules (which are to stage three what the control system dynamics are to stage two) includes the basis for a motor constancy mechanism.

Stage three, like stage two, also needs information about the effector system. However, whereas the information that stage two needs is about the spatial location of the effectors, stage three needs a detailed picture of their physical condition. It receives feedback about joint angles and prevailing levels of muscle tension. This information is presumably provided by proprioception, since no other source is evident.

Stage four. This is the last stage before the muscles go into action. Its output, the efferent neural signal (ENS), acts directly on the muscles and produces the effector modulation. The function of this stage is to expand the condensed form of the implicit response issuing from stage three into a real-time patterned sequence of efferent signals. These are transmitted to the muscles without further processing, but the pathways are not exactly straightforward. The muscle-spindle servo provides a final stabilization system that helps to compensate for factors threatening to disturb the desired relation between implicit response and muscular activity.

The dynamics of cat and mouse games

An analysis of two specific examples may help to illustrate the operation of this model. This time we shall use sober cartoon characters instead of drinking men. Let us see how these processing stages might operate in a series of Tom and Jerry episodes. Jerry is the psychologically sophisticated mouse who will survive because of his own superior knowledge rather than through his feline opponent's incompetence.

Scene 1. Jerry is at home. Tom lies in wait outside, patiently watching both of Jerry's two front doors, a paw raised above each. Jerry's speed on the ground is about par for a mouse but his escape is not assured by speed alone. If he emerges from either hole at full-speed Tom can respond quickly enough to catch him. Tom has a simple problem here since this is a two-choice reaction time situation in which the alternative paw-dropping responses can be programmed in advance. In the model, stage one defines paw-dropping and the required object modulation, and which in this case is the required effector modulation as well. The control system dynamics are simple and direct, the effector *is* the object. This direct relation ensures that stage two has no problems. However, stage three needs rules about what effect on the paw a particular implicit response (motor programme) will have. It also needs proprioceptive information from the paw and its leg so that appropriate motor constancy compensations can be made. The existing background muscle tension and the mechanical efficiency determined by the angles of the joint can then be compensated for in advance.

The cards seem stacked against Jerry unless he can come up with a plan for slowing down Tom's mouse-grabbing response. He conceives of two plans, both of which would have the

125

desired effect. The first simply requires making two more front-doors so turning Tom's original two-choice task into a four-choice task with the concomitant increase in response latency. Hopefully this would be sufficient to permit him to escape. Plan two is rather more subtle in form and avoids the gnawing involved in making additional exits. Jerry knows that Tom's stages two and three operate in such a way that once in action no new problem can be admitted until the previous one has been dealt with. Therefore, Jerry arranges a pendulum so that when it falls it makes a detached whisker, sacrificed for the purpose, protrude through one front door. He then lets go the pendulum and ten milliseconds after the whisker emerges, he dashes out the *other* hole. Tom, of course, registers the appearance of the whisker, interprets it as an indication of mouse to follow, and initiates the train of events leading to his paw descending. Tom's operational stages are committed by the time Jerry emerges through the other doorway. Tom's system can only process Jerry's escape after it has completed the specification of a fruitless grab at the mouseless-whisker. Jerry goes free, with acknowledgements to the psychological refractory period.

A more complex situation will serve to exemplify other functions of the system.

Scene 2. Tom is hanging by his toes from the picture rail above Jerry's front door. He is holding a golf-club which is long enough for him to be able to strike a mouse on the floor. Jerry is on the other side of the room planning how to get home with his head still attached to his body. Tom's plan is to swing the golf-club as Jerry makes for home and batter his rib-cage.

The main problem that Tom has is to time his response so that the head of the golf-club coincides with Jerry who is, of course, running full-tilt at right angles to its swing. In this situation the desired effect (from Tom's point of view) can be achieved by calling up a motor programme for swinging the golf-club and implementing it at the right time. So Tom spends some time practising his swing until the motor programme governing it is well established. The period of practice effectively deals in advance with the problem that stages two and three would otherwise have of formulating a motor programme to move the club-head from its initial position to the mouth of the mouse-hole. This problem is not trivial. The object in this

126

example is the club-head, the target is, of course, Jerry. Tom cannot see the club-head because he is watching Jerry, so the location of the object (the club-head) has to be inferred from a combination of proprioceptive information about the location of the handle of the golf-club and the known dimensions of its shaft. This inference is the province of stage one.

Stage two also has a more difficult problem since the relation between effectors (paws) and object (club-head) though direct is not simple. The control system dynamics in this case lack the overwhelming complexity of a third-order control system, but they do have to be known and used in defining the required effector modulation.

Tom's problems are not over. He is trying to hit a moving mouse, and even if Jerry runs in a straight line, there is still the problem of timing his swing so that he connects. He has to predict from his perception of mouse velocity when to initiate his swing. He needs to start the downward movement when the mouse is as many milliseconds away as the club-head will take to travel to the intended point of impact. Assessing velocity is a stage one problem but since movements cannot be corrected on the basis of visual information (about Jerry's approach velocity) within a quarter of a second of impact, stage three will need to specify the details of timing of the execution of the practised motor programme. This problem is bad enough supposing that Jerry runs at a constant speed. If however he accelerates at a constant rate (like the movement of an apple falling under the force of gravity) the prediction problem is even worse.

Given all of these complex computations one might be forgiven for suggesting that Jerry would be pretty safe trying a straight run and taking his chances. However, if one could generalize from cricketers to cartoon cats, such advice would not be sound. Tom's problem is somewhat easier than attempting to hook a bouncer from a fast bowler or hitting a baseball to left-field – and they are both done every day of the season. Jerry will need to use some guile to avoid involuntary aerobatics.

Suppose Jerry begins his run from across the room. If he runs at a constant velocity Tom can determine this and then predict ahead to the point at which he should begin his swing. Tom can monitor Jerry's approach and make a series of adjustments as the critical moment draws nearer. If Jerry maintains his speed his only salvation lies in the intrinsic inaccuracy of Tom's calculations. However, Jerry can almost certainly survive by altering his speed when he is within a quarter of a second of his front door. By this time Tom will be committed to his stroke and will miss – perhaps not by very much, but sufficient. Jerry will survive by making a correction necessary when it is too late to make any correction at all.

Inherited rules

Apart from emphasizing the differential operation of the model in particular, though fictional circumstances, these examples highlight one obvious feature. The final stages in the system are essentially less flexible in operation than the earlier stages. Considering them in reverse order, stage four is presumably 'wired-in' by the genetic code that governs development. This stage has to be a characteristic of all but the simplest species and has therefore had millions of years of evolution to bring it to a point of supreme efficiency. The elegance of the peripheral muscle-spindle servo is perhaps some indication of how well the system is designed. However, stage four is basically a passive interpreter expanding the implicit response into its real-time form and then producing the effector modulations that it defines.

Stage three has a more complex job to perform and one which depends upon building-in corrections for the prevailing and expected state of the effector system. It depends, implicitly, upon a set of rules which relate its output, the implicit response, to the feedback from the effectors about what that implicit response does to them. These are the effector anticipation rules, and without them the system would be hopelessly inefficient, thrashing around and governed only by a monitoring system that stopped it when, by accident, it produced the desired result.

These rules clearly have to be learned and, what is more, they have to be continuously relearned to take account of variations in the size and weight of the body. Adolescence is a critical period for stage three, because during this time there is a rapid change in muscle power, and in the mass and length of the limbs. Almost daily variations to the effector anticipation rules are necessary to maintain accurate assembly of implicit re-

128

sponses. It is no small wonder that adolescents frequently go through a phase of clumsiness which improves when their growth spurt ceases.

The initial stage of learning effector anticipation rules occurs in infancy. Until they have been learned the more elaborate kinds of response we have been discussing are inconceivable. No matter how brilliant his solutions to chess problems might be, the infant prodigy cannot break out of the fundamental limitations of his behaviour imposed by the level of maturity he has reached in developing his effector anticipation rules (see C2).

The simple skill of being able to throw stones at a target exemplifies the rapidity with which adjustments can be made to the effector anticipation rules. In this skill the muscular force which will be necessary to impart a particular velocity to the stone depends upon the mass which has to be accelerated. To reach a given velocity a larger force will have to be applied to a rock than to a pebble. As we know, long periods of recalibration of the effector anticipation rules are not required. An adjustment can be made very quickly on the basis of the perceived weight of the object.

Channels singular and plural

The stages hypothesized in this model require access to some kind of computing system to calculate the various outputs leading to an overt response. Defining a particular output as a required object modulation, and so on, says little or nothing about the nature of the processing system which produces it. So far, we have tried to give an initial specification of the sort of information each stage requires, the command signal which governs its operation and the operational rules upon which it depends. These vary from stage to stage. In this section an attempt will be made to describe the processing mechanism which subserves stages one and two. But first the reasons must be given for supposing that these stages have access to a mechanism which is different from that upon which stage three depends.

There are two main lines of argument that distinguish stage three. First, this stage makes use of rules which are general in their application, the effector anticipation rules. This contrasts with stages one and two where the rules governing the determination of the required object modulation, and subsequently the required effector modulation, are task dependent. In particular the control system dynamics relating effector change to object modulation are imposed by the control system which is an integral part of the task. It would seem plausible, therefore, that a more sophisticated and flexible processing mechanism would be needed for stages one and two than for stage three.

The second argument concerns the operating code of stage three. Both ROM and REM are plausibly specified in input (perceptual) codes. In fact, visual and proprioceptive feedback is the basis for monitoring that object and effector modulations have been appropriate. In contrast, the implicit response is most probably specified in an output (motor) code. A difference of operational code is another reason for supposing that different processing mechanisms are involved.

In addition to those arguments based on plausibility, there is one piece of empirical evidence which may give additional weight to the distinction. Leonard (1959) reported an experiment showing that if subjects had to respond with a finger to which a vibratory stimulus had been applied, a constant response latency was found. The 'typical' increase in reaction time with extent of choice did not emerge. It is tempting to speculate that in this experiment there was virtually direct entry to stage three, with the more usual processing leading to a specification of the ROM and REM being by-passed. If this view were correct, Leonard's data would give a nearly uncontaminated picture of the operation of stage three. The implications would be that stage three works on a response generation principle, with processing time taking a value that is hardly affected by response complexity. Stages one and two, however, appear to be governed by task complexity and, therefore, seem to work in a different way.

A multi-channel processor

Our view of the processing mechanism which serves stages one and two is based upon a modification of strict single channel theory. In one sense such a theory is untenable from the start. The processing necessary to maintain blood pressure and blood oxygen levels continues throughout all sorts of other activities of a demanding nature. Whatever the limitations of single channel operation they do not extend to the monitoring and control of vegetative functions. This would suggest that some

130

kinds of information are processed in special sorts of channels, channels which can only deal with particular sorts of information. Our view is an extension of this and postulates several special-purpose channels nested beneath one super-channel at the top of the hierarchy. These views are related to those advanced by Kerr (1973) and Shallice (1972) as well as Allport *et al.* (1972).

We suggest there are three levels of information processing channel. At the top is the super-channel, at the bottom the wired-in genetically determined channels subserving vegetative functions, and in between a set of channels that are more or less dependent upon learning. Their function is determined by software rather than hardware, to borrow a computing analogy. The super-channel and the mid-level channels are the ones most important for the control of behaviour. The special feature of the single super-channel is its almost unlimited flexibility and adaptiveness. It is in this channel that problem-solving is accommodated – at least when it is accomplished at the level of conscious awareness (see A7). The special-purpose channels below are limited in the situations that they can deal with, though extremely efficient in handling problems within their competence.

There are a number of features of the multi-channel model. A particular problem may be within the competence of a lower level channel, and all problems are within the competence of the super-channel. It follows that the processing system could be dealing with the same problem in two different ways, simultaneously. The disadvantage of the super-channel is that as a consequence of its extreme flexibility it is slower in processing a problem than is a special-purpose channel set up for and only capable of dealing with that kind of problem. The danger of falling headlong down the stairs when one deliberately attends to one's feet may illustrate the interference of the super-channel in a skill perfectly adequately performed by a special-purpose channel.

Each channel is considered to be limited in its processing performance. Each is a limited channel. Essentially all channels are limited quantitatively, for example in the speed with which they can process information. In addition, the special-purpose channels are limited qualitatively. Each can process only a certain kind of information, and in a particular way.

It is a basic assumption that one of the consequences of

acquiring skill is the establishment of special-purpose channels for handling the necessary computations. Before skill is acquired, if these computations are to be done at all they have to be done by the super-channel. Once a suitably programmed special-purpose channel has been established it will be the most efficient way of handling information. However, under certain circumstances the limits of competence of the special-purpose channel may be exceeded and then, once again, recourse must be had to the super-channel. If at the time of this crisis the the super-channel was busy doing something more intellectual, the crisis would dominate and the intellectual activity would be interrupted. Riding a bicycle normally depends on a special-purpose channel processing. This leaves the super-channel free to contemplate the rights of man or the third law of thermo-dynamics. A sudden change of traffic or a very uneven road-surface will usually be enough to wipe the mind clean of these esoteric contemplations.

We are postulating that stages one and two of our model have access to this multi-channel processor. Let us explore its operation in the context of the evidence pointing to single channel operation and discussed in Chapter 7. In particular we shall consider the psychological refractory period data, the inter-mittent correction of continuous movements and performance on two simultaneous tasks.

PRP revisited

The data from experiments on the psychological refractory period (PRP) show in general that when two reaction time tasks are presented in quick succession one takes precedence. How-ever, this may not be complete as shown by the need to con-sider a time-sharing system so that both tasks get processed within the same epoch. These arguments will not be repeated in this chapter.

It might be thought somewhat peculiar to find *any* evidence for single channel operation if the processor is of this multi-channel kind. We argue the contrary. There are a limited number of special-purpose channels each programmed to carry out a specific calculation. If two tasks require access to the same special-purpose channel because they entail the same calculation, a bottleneck problem may arise. The only situation that would be free from this problem would be if the two tasks were so differ-ent that they had no computational requirements in common.

Most PRP experiments use pairs of either simple or choice reaction time tasks. They usually require subjects to respond manually to both tasks and the stimuli have more often than not been presented visually. Multi-channel theory suggests that if two tasks can be found which are very different from one another, and if they were combined in the standard psychological refractory period paradigm, the usual delay to the processing of the second signal should be absent. Essentially this experiment has been done by Greenwald and Shulman (1973) who found no evidence of the PRP effect when one task was moving a lever in the direction shown by an illuminated arrow, and the other task was simply saying a letter that was heard. These tasks differ in many ways, with respect to modality of stimulus presentation, mode of response, and the implication of a linguistic coding system. The results show that these differences were sufficient to eliminate the normal delay.

Multi-channel theory would not require that the two tasks had nothing in common, just that they should have insufficient common elements to give rise to a queuing problem at one or more special-purpose channels.

This example of the use of the multi-channel processor draws out another of its characteristics. If each special-purpose channel is tailored for a specific type of calculation, it follows that for all but the simplest processing problems several passes through the processor will be required, making use of different special-purpose channels on each pass. This highlights the decomposition of skill tasks that was implicit in the time sharing explanation of the non-unit negative slope and the effects of a second signal on the latency of the first response.

One might ask why, if the super-channel can do *any* computation, the second arriving task could not be dealt with at top level while the first task received priority treatment below. There is no constraint in the model's operation to prevent this but the relative slowness of the super-channel would probably make this kind of split-processing less efficient than waiting for the appropriate high speed special-purpose channel to become free.

Further intermittent corrections
Intermittent modulation of responses in tracking tasks has often been attributed, in the past, to the same underlying cause

as the psychological refractory period effect. We take the view that the intermittency effect may be, in part, accounted for in these terms but it is mainly due to something quite different. Intermittency arises because the system needs to operate in terms of the future rather than reactively to the present. The problem is that in order to hit a moving target a response has to be computed which takes account of where the target will be when that response is executed. The obvious problem is to avoid using out-of-date information in computing the response. This may be overcome by predicting ahead a future position of the target, but there is the problem of choosing how far ahead in time to predict.

Ideally the system would need to know how long it was going to take to do its computations. If this time was known, this would also be the optimal time ahead to predict. However, it seems most unlikely that this computation time can be known until the computations have been completed. The problem that this presents may be avoided if the system implements responses at fixed times. The time for the next response is then predictable and, likewise, the appropriate time ahead to predict the future position of the target is also determined. This scheme would result in regular intermittent corrections in a continuous task such as tracking, and this is exactly what is observed.

Doing two tasks at once
Dual-task performance has provided perhaps the most difficult data for single channel theory to handle. Both Shaffer (1975) and Allport *et al.* (1972) have reported experiments in which subjects performed two tasks concurrently without any re-duction in performance on either task. Both reports also include accounts of experiments in which the combination of two tasks produced the more usually observed mutual interference be-tween the tasks. It appears from these reports that to avoid mutual interference between the tasks it is necessary for the tasks to be very well practised and as dissimilar as possible. For example, Allport finds no interference between sight-reading music and shadowing, and Shaffer demonstrated that a very highly skilled visual copy-typist could shadow at the same time as she was typing without any impairment of performance.

The multi-channel processor would be expected to serve two tasks at once (or even more) provided that special-purpose subordinate channels had been established by practice and that there was no competition between the tasks for the use of the same special-purpose channels. These two conditions are only likely to prevail when both tasks are highly practised and when they are dissimilar. Otherwise, if the tasks share the same special-purpose channels there will be some degree of congestion at one or more of the subordinate channels with a consequential deterioration of performance on one or both tasks.

Information traffic control. It is interesting to speculate about what might limit the number of things that could be done simultaneously. One factor would be the number of special-purpose channels and the variety of the tasks necessary to avoid competition for the same channel during processing. However, another problem has been reviewed by Moray (1967), who notes that in some experiments subjects instructed to divide their attention between two sources seem to lose some of their processing capacity as a result. He concludes that this 'lost' capacity has been absorbed by a process devoted to directing information traffic.

A similar theoretical problem arises in the operation of the multi-channel processor. Some system has to direct a problem to one channel rather than another, and there is a very real danger that a little 'man in the mind' might get the job (see A1). There is no solution to this traffic control problem, at present. In many respects the problem looks rather like the problem of devising a mechanism to account for selective attention. Perhaps a similar mechanism will have application to this problem as well.

Consciousness and the super-channel

It is a feature of tasks which are, as yet, poorly learned that subjects seek to guide their performance by the explicit use of verbal rules. We discussed the use of verbal guidance in Chapter 8. In developing the model at the beginning of this chapter we noted that stages one and two depend heavily on the use of rules, and the rules governing the activity of these two stages, unlike those at stage three, may very well be available in a conscious verbal form. As practice proceeds and the task becomes more 'automatic' these verbal rules give way to others not accessible to conscious report. This change would seem to be quite satisfactorily accounted for in terms of the development of special-purpose subordinate processing channels, the initial performance being largely due to the intervention of the super-channel.

Putting these trends together it is tempting to identify the contents of the super-channel with the contents of consciousness. It is part of our conceptualization of the super-channel that it is reserved for difficult processing jobs for which no special-purpose subsidiary exists. It is also the region where verbal control of behaviour operates. However, it is not assumed that it is empty whenever these difficult problems are absent, though what determines its contents is a difficult problem.

This identification of the super-channel with consciousness has a number of consequences. One of these is to underline the potentially misleading quality of introspective reports about how some particular performance is achieved. We have noted that the super-channel could be working on the same problem as a subordinate special-purpose channel. However, it is not necessarily the case that the two channels would be dealing with the problem in the same way, even if the end result was the same. This raises the possibility that performance might be determined by the subordinate channel while introspection was based on the 'irrelevant' activity of the super-channel.

One final point. James (1890) emphasized the unitary nature of consciousness, and this characteristic has seldom been questioned since. The multi-channel processor might be thought to deny this quality by allowing several different things to be processed at the same time. This potential difficulty is avoided by having an appropriate rule mapping consciousness onto some particular feature of the processing system. It is not the only way of achieving this end, but mapping consciousness onto the super-channel is one way of reflecting James' view of the last century in the information-processing context of this one.

Further Reading

The following is a selection of books concerned with skill psychology, or particular issues in it:

Annett, J. (1969) *Feedback and Human Behaviour*. Harmondsworth: Penguin.

Fitts, P. M. and Posner, M. I. (1967) *Human Performance*. Belmont, Calif.: Brooks-Cole.

Holding, D. H. (1965) *Principles of Training*. Oxford: Pergamon.

Keele, S. W. (1973) *Attention and Human Performance*. Pacific Palisades, Calif.: Goodyear.

Legge, D. (ed.) (1970) *Skills: Selected Readings*. Harmondsworth: Penguin.

Welford, A. T. (1968) *Fundamentals of Skill*. London: Methuen.

Applications of the psychology of perceptual-motor skill features substantively in some areas of applied psychology and in the specialist discipline, ergonomics. Here are some texts that consider these applications:

Holding, D. H. (ed.) (1969) *Experimental Psychology in Industry: Selected Readings*. Harmondsworth: Penguin.

Murrell, K. F. H. (1965) *Ergonomics: Man in His Working Environment*. London: Chapman and Hall.

Murrell, K. F. H. (1975) *Men and Machines*. Essential Psychology E4. London: Methuen.

Singleton, W. T. (1974) *Man-Machine Systems*. Harmondsworth: Penguin.

Warr, P. B. (ed.) (1971) *Psychology at Work*. Harmondsworth: Penguin.

References and Name Index

The numbers in italics following each entry
refer to page numbers within this book.

Adams, J. A. (1971) A closed-loop theory of motor learning. *Journal of Motor Behaviour 3*: 111–49. *114, 115–17*

Allport, D. A., Antonis, B. and Reynolds, P. (1972) On the division of attention: a disproof of the single channel hypothesis. *Quarterly Journal of Experimental Psychology 24*: 225–35. *106–7, 134*

Annett, J. (1969) *Feedback and Human Behaviour*. Harmondsworth: Penguin. *112*

Bartlett, F. C. (1947) The measurement of human skill. *British Medical Journal i*: 835–8 and 877–80. *116*

Bartlett, F. C. (1958) *Thinking, An Experimental and Social Study*. London: Allen and Unwin. *7*

Begbie, G. H. (1959) Accuracy in aiming in linear hand movements. *Quarterly Journal of Experimental Psychology 11*: 65–75. *74*

Beggs, W. D. A. and Howarth, C. I. (1970) Movement control in a repetitive motor task. *Nature 225*: 752–3. *50, 66, 75*

Briggs, G. E. (1964) The generality of research on transfer functions. In A. W. Melton (ed.) *Categories of Human Learning*. New York: Academic Press. *119*

Briggs, G. E. (1974) On the predictor variable for choice reaction time. *Memory and Cognition 2*: 575–80. *35*

Broadbent, D. E. (1958) *Perception and Communication*. Oxford: Pergamon. *99*

Broadbent, D. E. and Gregory, M. (1967) Psychological refractory period and the length of time required to make a decision. *Proceedings of the Royal Society*, Series B, *168*: 181–93. *98, 104*

Bryan, W. L. and Harter, N. (1899) Studies on the telegraphic language: the acquisition of a hierarchy of habits. *Psychological Review 6*, 345–75. *118*

Chomsky, N. (1959) Review of Skinner's *Verbal Behaviour*. *Language 35*: 26–58. *20, 113*

Craik, K. J. W. (1947) Theory of the human operator in control systems. I. The operator as an engineering system. *British Journal of Psychology 38*: 56–61. *51, 90*

Crossman, E. R. F. W. (1953) Entropy and choice time: the effect of frequency unbalance on choice-response. *Quarterly Journal of Psychology 5*: 41–51. *33, 43*

Crossman, E. R. F. W. (1959) A theory of the acquisition of speed-skill. *Ergonomics 2*: 153–66. *110*

Deutsch, J. A. and Deutsch, D. (1963) Attention: some theoretical considerations. *Psychological Review 70*: 80–90. *99*

Donders, F. C. (1868) Die Schnelligkeit psychischer Processe. *Archiv fur Anatomie und Physiologie* 657–81. *23–5*

Drury, C. G. (1971) Movements with lateral constraint. *Ergonomics 14*: 293–305. *75–6*

Fitts, P. M. (1954) The information capacity of the human motor system in controlling the amplitude of movement. *Journal of Experimental Psychology 47*: 381–91. *61*

Fitts, P. M. and Peterson, J. R. (1964) Information capacity of discrete motor responses. *Journal of Experimental Psychology 67*: 103–12. *62*

Fitts, P. M. and Posner, M. I. (1967) *Human Performance.* Belmont, Calif.: Brooks-Cole. *40*

Fitts, P. M. and Seeger, C. M. (1953) S-R compatibility: spatial characteristics of stimulus and response codes. *Journal of Experimental Psychology 46*: 199–210. *38*

Fleishman, E. A. and Rich, S. (1963) Role of kinaesthetic and spatial-visual abilities in perceptual-motor learning. *Journal of Experimental Psychology 66*: 6–11. *117*

Fuchs, A. H. (1962) The progression–regression hypotheses in perceptual-motor skill learning. *Journal of Experimental Psychology 63*: 177–82. *119*

Gibbs, C. B. (1970) Servo-control systems in organisms and the transfer of skill. In D. Legge (ed.) *Skills: Selected Readings.* Harmondsworth: Penguin. *73*

Greenwald, A. G. and Shulman, H. G. (1973) On doing two things at once: II. Elimination of the psychological refractory period effect. *Journal of Experimental Psychology 101*: 70–6. *133*

Gregory, R. L. (1966) *Eye and Brain.* London: Weidenfeld and Nicolson. *54*

Helmholtz, H. von (1850) On the methods of measuring very small portions of time, and their applications to physiological processes. *Philosophical Magazine 6*: 313–25. *22–4*

Herman, L. M. and McCauley, M. E. (1969) Delay in responding to the first stimulus in the 'psychological refractory period' experiment. *Journal of Experimental Psychology 81*: 344–50. *105*

Hick, W. E. (1952) On the rate of gain of information. *Quarterly Journal of Experimental Psychology 4*: 11–26. *29, 32–4, 41, 43*

Holding, D. H. (1965) *Principles of Training.* Oxford: Pergamon. *110, 112*

Howard, I. P. and Templeton, W. B. (1966) *Human Spatial Orientation.* London: John Wiley. *55*

Howarth, C. I., Beggs, W. D. A. and Bowden, J. (1971) The relationship between speed and accuracy of movement aimed at a target. *Acta Psychologica 35*: 207–18. *76*

Hyman, R. (1953) Stimulus information as a determinant of reaction time. *Journal of Experimental Psychology 45*: 188–96. *33*

James, W. (1890) *The Principles of Psychology.* New York: Holt. *117, 136*

Johnson, H. W. (1961) Skills = speed × accuracy × form × adaptability. *Perceptual and Motor Skills 13*: 163–70. *13*

Jones, B. (1974) Is proprioception important for skilled performance? *Journal of Motor Behaviour* 6: 33–45. *54*

Keele, S. W. (1968) Movement control in skilled motor performance. *Psychological Bulletin* 70: 387–403. *64–5, 75, 114*

Keele, S. W. and Posner, M. I. (1968) Processing of visual feedback in rapid movements. *Journal of Experimental Psychology* 77: 155–8. *49, 65–6*

Keller, F. S. (1959) The phantom plateau. *Journal of the Experimental Analysis of Behaviour* 1: 1–13. *118*

Kerr, B. (1973) Processing demands during mental operations. *Memory and Cognition* 1: 401–12. *131*

Kirkby, C. (1974) Hick's Law revisited. *Acta Psychologica* 38: 277–82. *45*

Lashley, K. S. (1951) The problem of serial order in behaviour. In L. A. Jeffress (ed.) *Cerebral Mechanisms in Behaviour, The Hixon Symposium.* New York: John Wiley. *114*

Legge, D. and Pottinger, J. M. (1968) Is there a motor constancy mechanism? *British Journal of Psychology* 59: 349–59. *58*

Leonard, J. A. (1959) Tactual choice reactions. *Quarterly Journal of Experimental Psychology* 11: 76–83. *37–8, 101, 130*

Merkel, J. (1885) Die zeitlichen Verhaltnisse der Willensthätigkeit. *Philosophie Studion* 2: 73–127. *29, 32*

Miller, G. A., Galanter, E. and Pribram, K. (1960). *Plans and the Structure of Behaviour.* New York: Holt. *112*

Moray, N. (1967) Where is capacity limited? A survey and a model. *Acta Psychologica* 27: 84–92. *135*

Morin, R. E. and Forrin, B. (1963) Response equivocation and reaction time. *Journal of Experimental Psychology* 66: 30–6. *34*

Mowbray, G. H. (1960) Choice reaction times for skilled responses. *Quarterly Journal of Experimental Psychology* 12: 193–202. *101*

Mowbray, G. H. and Rhoades, M. V. (1959) On the reduction of choice reaction times with practice. *Quarterly Journal of Experimental Psychology* 11: 16–23. *37–9, 45, 101*

Neisser, U. (1963) Decision-time without reaction time: experiments in visual scanning. *American Journal of Psychology* 76: 376–85. *101*

Neisser, U. (1967) *Cognitive Psychology.* New York: Appleton-Century-Crofts. *102*

Poulton, E. C. (1957) On prediction in skilled movements. *Psychological Bulletin* 54: 467–78. *91, 115*

Poulton, E. C. (1974) *Tracking Skill and Manual Control.* London: Academic Press. *80–1*

Rabbitt, P. M. A. (1966) Errors and error correction in choice-response tasks. *Journal of Experimental Psychology* 71: 264–72. *67*

Seibel, R. (1963) Discrimination reaction time for a 1023-alternative task. *Journal of Experimental Psychology* 66: 215–26. *45*

Shaffer, L. H. (1975) Multiple attention in continuous verbal tasks. In P. M. A. Rabbitt and S. Dornic (eds) *Attention and Performance, V.* London: Academic Press. *107, 134*

Shallice, T. (1972) Dual functions of consciousness. *Psychological Review* 79: 383–93. *131*

Shannon, C. E. and Weaver, W. (1949) *The Mathematical Theory of Communication.* Urbana: University of Illinois Press. *29*

Sherrington, C. S. (1906) On the proprioceptive system, especially its reflex aspect. *Brain* 29: 467–82. *54*

Skinner, B. F. (1957) *Verbal Behaviour.* New York: Appleton-Century-Crofts. *20, 113*

Smith, E. E. (1968) Choice reaction times: an analysis of the major theoretical positions. *Psychological Bulletin 69*: 77–110. *43*

Smith, M. C. (1967) Theories of the psychological refractory period. *Psychological Bulletin 67*: 202–13. *97*

Sternberg, S. (1969) The discovery of processing stages: extensions of Donders' method. In W. G. Koster (ed.) *Attention and Performance, II*. Amsterdam: North Holland. *25–8*

Sternberg, S. (1975) Memory scanning: new findings and current controversies. *Quarterly Journal of Experimental Psychology 27*: 1–32. *25–8*

Theios, J. and Falmagne, J.-C. (1971) A probabilistic push-down stack model for the organization of short-term memory in stimulus identification and prediction experiments. Paper presented to Mathematical Psychology Meetings, Princeton, September 1971. *44*

Theios, J., Smith, P. G., Haviland, S. E., Traupmann, J. and Moy, M. C. (1973) Memory scanning as a serial self-terminating process. *Journal of Experimental Psychology 97*: 323–36. *44*

Treisman, A. M. (1964) Selective attention in man. *British Medical Bulletin 20*: 12–16. *99*

Triggs, T. J. (1968) Capacity sharing and speeded reactions to successive signals. *Technical Report 9*, University of Michigan, Contract No. AF 49(678)-1736. US Department of Defence. *104*

Vince, M. A. (1948) Intermittency of control movements and the psychological refractory period. *British Journal of Psychology 38*: 149–57. *90*

Way, T. C. and Gottsdanker, R. (1968) Psychological refractoriness with varying differences between tasks. *Journal of Experimental Psychology 78*: 38–45. *104*

Welford, A. T. (1958) *Ageing and Human Skill*. London: Oxford University Press. *17*

Welford, A. T. (1968) *Fundamentals of Skill*. London: Methuen. *41*

Whitman, C. P. and Geller, E. S. (1972) Prediction outcome and choice reaction time: stimulus versus response anticipation. *Journal of Experimental Psychology 93*: 193–7. *44*

Woodworth, R. S. (1899) The accuracy of voluntary movement. *Psychological Review Monograph Supplements* 3, No. 3. *48*

Subject Index